IMPERIAL PALACE

AUTO COLLECTION

CONTENTS

INTRODUCTION

■ When I bought my first car in 1949, at the age of nineteen, I obviously had no inkling that one day I would own more automobiles than I could keep track of. The thought that I, thirty years down the road, would build a museum to display a portion of my cars, and that it would take half a dozen warehouses to store the rest, would have seemed preposterous to me at the time. ■ That first automobile, a 1939 Ford two-door sedan, was not an object that I cherished for its mechanical sophistication—that part of the car was probably not overly impressive, anyway. As a matter of fact, I spent very little time under its hood; between school and work—I've had a steady job since I was thirteen—there was simply no time. ■ Among other automobiles that I remember well was the one my wife Betty—she has been by my side since 1954—and I owned when we were married, a 1951 Pontiac two-door sedan. It seems the car people drive as newlyweds is the one they most often recall with nostalgia—that and the first car they ever drove. ■ I'm not sure why I favored Pontiac in those days. Perhaps it was because my father—a man I admired immensely—always drove Pontiacs. Or perhaps it was simply because of that catchy slogan, "Dollar for dollar, you can't beat a Pontiac." ■ My many years in the construction business made me appreciate the versatility of the pickup truck, and I have owned and

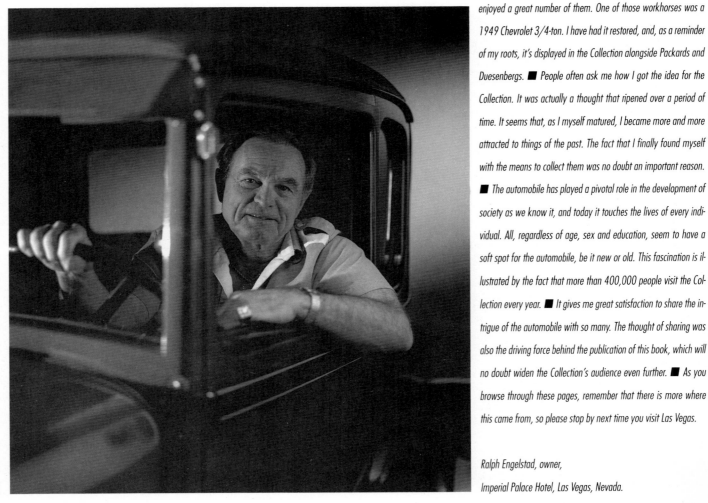

enjoyed a great number of them. One of those workhorses was a 1949 Chevrolet 3/4-ton. I have had it restored, and, as a reminder of my roots, it's displayed in the Collection alongside Packards and Duesenbergs. ■ People often ask me how I got the idea for the Collection. It was actually a thought that ripened over a period of time. It seems that, as I myself matured, I became more and more attracted to things of the past. The fact that I finally found myself with the means to collect them was no doubt an important reason. ■ The automobile has played a pivotal role in the development of society as we know it, and today it touches the lives of every individual. All, regardless of age, sex and education, seem to have a soft spot for the automobile, be it new or old. This fascination is illustrated by the fact that more than 400,000 people visit the Collection every year. ■ It gives me great satisfaction to share the intrigue of the automobile with so many. The thought of sharing was also the driving force behind the publication of this book, which will no doubt widen the Collection's audience even further. ■ As you browse through these pages, remember that there is more where this came from, so please stop by next time you visit Las Vegas.

Ralph Engelstad, owner,
Imperial Palace Hotel, Las Vegas, Nevada.

PART ONE

THE COLLECTION

■ The Imperial Palace employs the latest in visual communications technology to promote the Collection's virtues. The photo sequence below captures one of three 700-square-foot electronic message boards strategically located on the facades of the hotel so as to catch the attention of the ever-flowing foot and wheel traffic that travels the Strip. Their 25,000 multicolored light bulbs—drawing electricity at the rate of 300 amps each—illuminate the Las Vegas skyline day and night.

■ The initial steps on the road that led to the formation of Imperial Palace Auto Collection, as with all beginnings, were modest ones. The tentative nature of these early efforts are illustrated by the fact that when Ralph Engelstad bought his first collector car, a 1929 Ford Model A Roadster, the motivations guiding his purchase—as well as the intended focus of the museum he planned to build—were completely different from those that directed the building of the Collection as it stands today. ■ Consistent with Engelstad's vision, that first Ford, purchased in March 1979 and pictured with Engelstad on page 6, was meant to form the nucleus of an exhibit featuring Fords exclusively. His plan called for the acquisition of one example of every model and year produced by the manufacturer, some 241 automobiles in all, according to Engelstad's calculations. ■ For a long time, however, the lone Ford constituted the entire range of the Collection. With Engelstad's time occupied organizing the expansion of the hotel and casino, plans for the museum had to take a back seat, and Engelstad didn't get around to buying his second Ford until November 1980. ■ From then on, however, Engelstad devoted more time to the museum project and soon became a familiar sight at collector car auctions around the country. Additional Fords soon joined the initial two, among them a 1919 Model T, a 1928 Model A depot hack

■ With five twenty-story towers—one of which forms the backdrop in the photograph below—and a total of 2700 rooms, the Imperial Palace is the largest privately owned hotel in the world. As such, it is in a unique position to draw visitors to the Collection. No less than 400,000 tour the 65,000-square-foot facility each year, making it one of the world's most popular automotive museums. The 1936 Mercedes-Benz Spezial-Roadster pictured here has come to represent the spirit of the Collection.

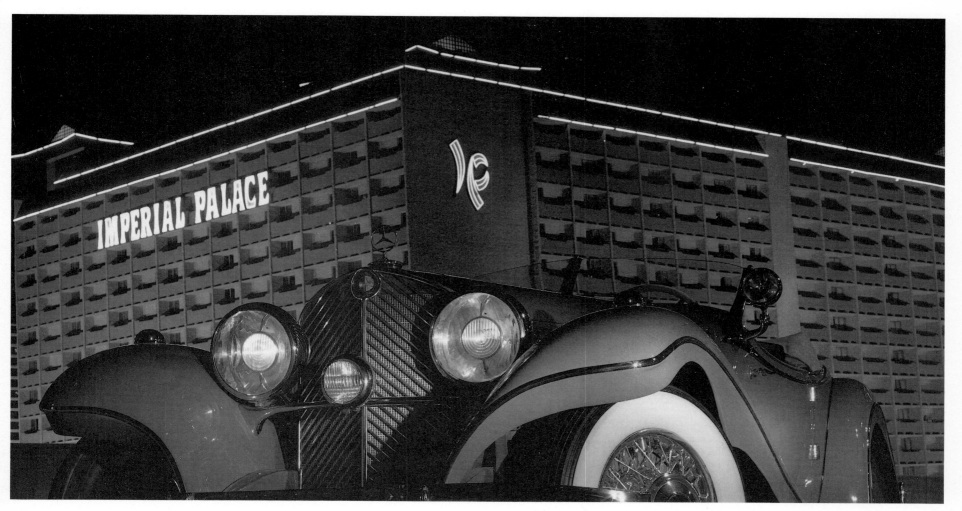

■ These scenes, featuring some of the Collection's many dioramas, were photographed at night when visitors would not obscure them. The ghostly darkness is given further drama by costumed mannequins, who at times seem to come alive. Below, one area of the Collection features a farm scene, with a 1919 Ford Model T delivery truck as its main attraction. A number of cars are displayed with their hoods open; at the top of the page, a 1937 Cord 812 and a 1957 Thunderbird show off their potent engines.

■ The initial steps on the road that led to the formation of Imperial Palace Auto Collection, as with all beginnings, were modest ones. The tentative nature of these early efforts are illustrated by the fact that when Ralph Engelstad bought his first collector car, a 1929 Ford Model A Roadster, the motivations guiding his purchase—as well as the intended focus of the museum he planned to build—were completely different from those that directed the building of the Collection as it stands today. ■ Consistent with Engelstad's vision, that first Ford, purchased in March 1979 and pictured with Engelstad on page 8, was meant to form the nucleus of an exhibit featuring Fords exclusively. His plan called for the acquisition of one example of every model and year produced by the manufacturer, some 241 automobiles in all, according to Engelstad's calculations. ■ For a long time, however, the lone Ford constituted the entire range of the Collection. With Engelstad's time occupied organizing the expansion of the hotel and casino, plans for the museum had to take a back seat, and Engelstad didn't get around to buying his second Ford until November 1980. ■ From then on, however, Engelstad devoted more time to the museum project and soon became a familiar sight at collector car auctions around the country. Additional Fords soon joined the initial two, among them a 1919 Model T, a 1928 Model A depot hack

■ *In the illustration at the bottom of the previous page, Henry Ford himself is seen pondering*

the underhood simplicity of his Model T, its four-cylinder engine in this case providing motive power for a 1917 tanker truck.

The large illustration on this page recreates a scene from the fairy-tale life of the King of Siam, whose

1928 Delage occupies the center stage. Many displays have colorful murals painted on the wall behind them,

depicting scenes relating to the automobile they accompany.

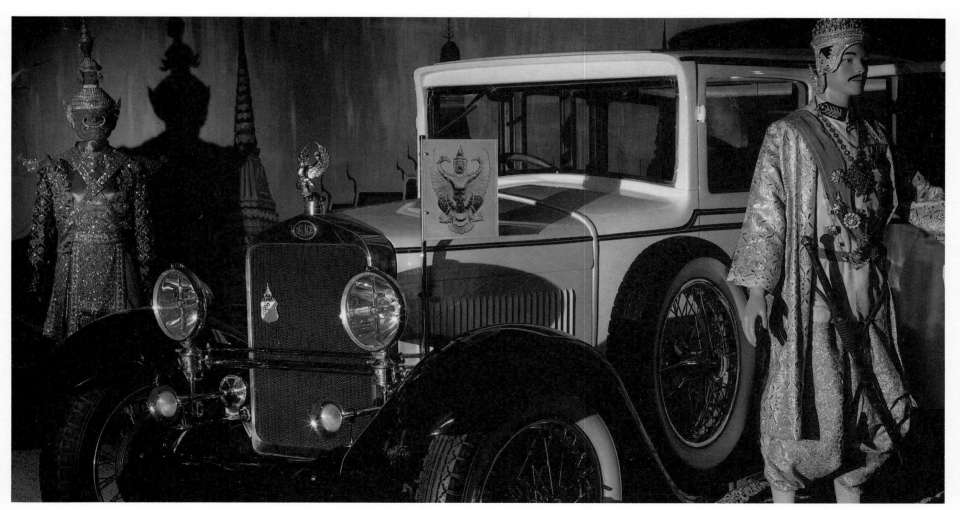

■ Below, two of the numerous military vehicles contained in the Collection. The image of power and simplicity presented by the front end of a 1940 Dodge Command Car is indicative of the strength that helped America win World War II. At the top of the page, a curious vehicle from the other side, the German Kettenrad, a small, track-type personnel carrier. Other military exhibits range from a German Krausse Maffei—the largest personnel carrier ever built—to an American paratrooper's lightweight bicycle.

nent home for the Collection became increasingly urgent. Engelstad's plan for such a facility called for the top floor of the five-story Imperial Palace parking structure to be enclosed, creating a 65,000-square-foot area that would allow the exhibition of approximately 200 cars. ■ The grand opening of the Imperial Palace Auto Collection took place on the last day of November 1981, in a festive celebration attended by local dignitaries that culminated in Engelstad's wielding scissors to cut the traditional ribbon. ■ The man whose ambition had made the Collection a reality, Ralph Engelstad, was born in Thief River Falls, Minnesota, in 1930. One day in 1948, when Engelstad, fresh out of high school, labored at his part-time job unloading boxcars in Grand Forks, a co-worker—who happened to be a university professor—encouraged him to attend college, an eventuality that until then had not been included in the young man's still-diffuse master plan for his life. A hockey scholarship—Engelstad was already an accomplished goalie—made the college option a reality. ■ At one point tempted by an offer to join the Chicago Blackhawks as a professional player, Engelstad instead opted for the more prudent choice of starting his own construction company, a move made possible thanks to a $2500 loan from Valley Bank of Grand Forks, North Dakota, a local bank with a nose for budding potential. ■ In the

■ Pictured here is that portion of the Collection devoted to fire apparatus. Its centerpiece is a massive

1913 Seagrave pumper, which is joined by a 1915 Ford LaFrance ladder truck. At the bottom of the previous page is a

1927 Harley-Davidson, one of a number of motorcycles on display. Additional two-wheelers include a rare

1908 Experiment, a quartet of handsome Pierce-Arrows, a handful of Indians—among them the 1947 model once

owned by actor Steve McQueen—and a 1955 Ariel, the British thoroughbred.

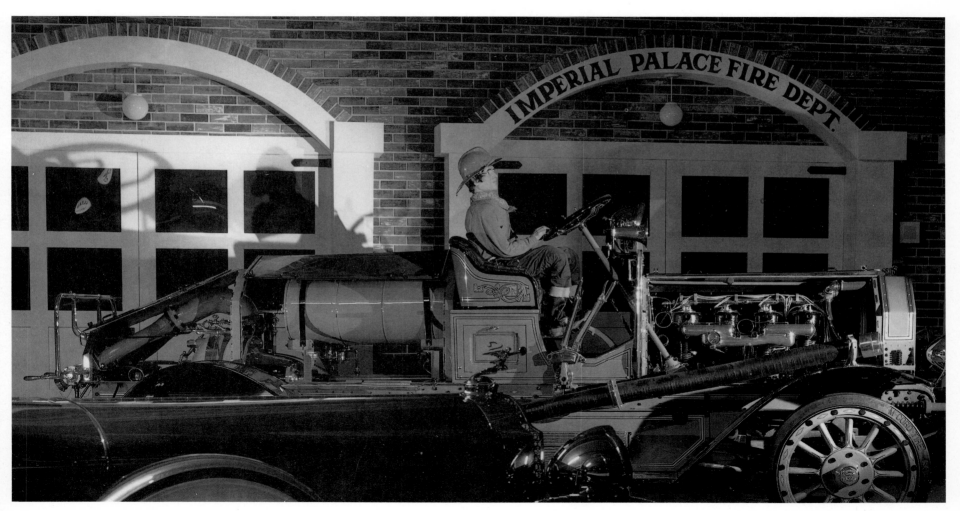

■ With its inventory of vehicles exceeding 600—and still growing—the Collection is forced

to house many of its automobiles in auxiliary storage areas prior to their restoration or display. Seen on these pages are

glimpses of the Rolls-Royce and Mercedes-Benz holdings—two of the largest concentrations of these

marques in the world. The Rolls-Royces, which currently number more than fifty, are mostly American-built. Among

these, a 1930 Phantom I "Beetleback" by Brewster stands out as one of the finest.

course of the next decade—a portion of which he still spent in school—Engelstad went from erecting farm storage buildings in the State of North Dakota to building complete housing projects. The young entrepreneur invested his earnings in land and apartment complexes, but when, in the late Fifties, the bottom fell out of the local economy, he sold his holdings and moved west to booming Las Vegas. ■ During the next half-dozen years, Engelstad erected tract housing in Las Vegas as well as numerous commercial buildings at the Nevada Test Site. In 1965, he bought the Thunderbird Air Field, only to turn around and sell it to Howard Hughes two years later—a deal that facilitated an expansion to the famed Strip, although at its out-of-the-mainstream south end, where Engelstad bought the 116-room Kona Kai, later to become the Klondike. From his new vantage point, Engelstad appraised a move to a more advantageous spot on the Strip. The opportunity finally presented itself in 1971, when the 176-room Flamingo Capri—strategically located opposite Caesar's Palace—came on the market. ■ Engelstad soon discovered that, due to the disproportionately high value of the land, earnings from the hotel operation hardly paid its property taxes—prompting a choice between selling or building. With construction being Engelstad's primary business, his choice of the latter seemed obvious. Today, follow-

■ In the scene below, a 1936 Mercedes-Benz 500K Spezial-Roadster divides two rows of Mercedes-Benz and Rolls-Royce automobiles. The Spezial-Roadster, with its stunning combination of beauty and performance, was one of the most breathtaking bodystyles to emerge from any European automaker or coachbuilder during the late Thirties. Another Daimler-Benz milestone of the period was the monumental 770K, of which the Collection owns a large number, a few of which are lined up here form a backdrop to the Spezial-Roadster.

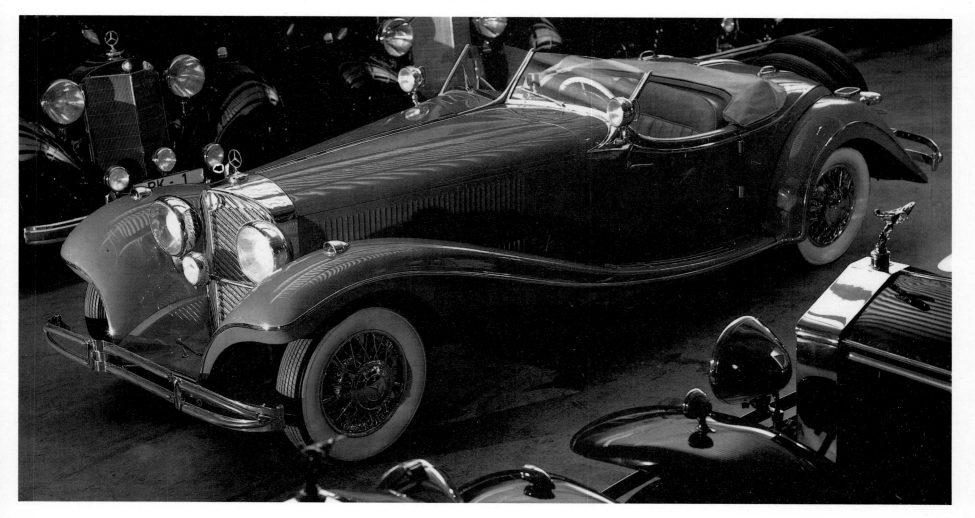

■ Illustrated on this page is the Collection's restoration shop, a 25,000-square-foot facility encompassing separate areas for bodywork, upholstery repair and mechanical repair. Below, dramatic stage illumination raises the highlights of a partially restored Mercedes-Benz 770K. Its gleaming engine stands finished, while its chassis awaits the completion of the fenders and hood. A number of demanding, ground-up restorations have been executed here, the Collection's Mercedes-Benz G4 among the most difficult.

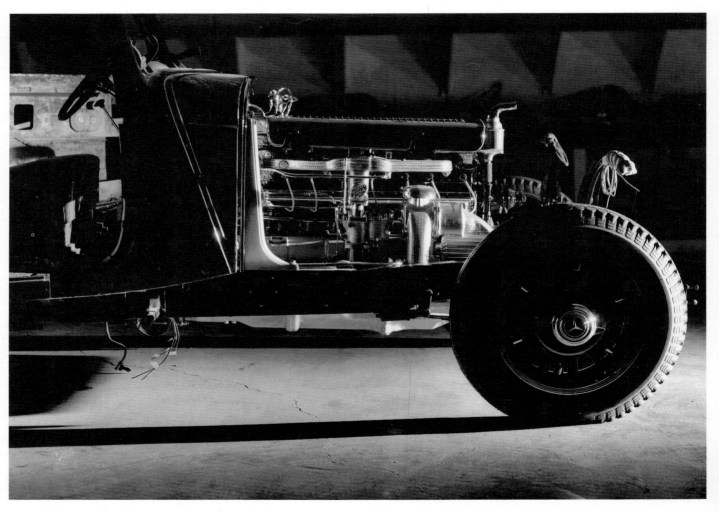

ing a succession of expansions, the Imperial Palace and its five towers can accommodate as many as 5300 guests—a capacity that currently ranks it as the eighth largest hotel in the world. Through it all, Engelstad has held on to his sole ownership of the huge complex, allowing him to follow a course of independence; Imperial Palace remains the only privately owned major hotel on the Las Vegas strip. ■ Richie Clyne, the Collection's administrator since its inception shared his boss's appetite for Fords. In Clyne's case, it all began with a 1930 Model A he bought as a twelve-year old living on New York's Long Island. ■ Clyne's interest in vintage machinery eventually led him to a career in auto mechanics. He still could not get enough of automobiles, however, and began restoring collector cars in his spare time. The hobby soon led to a pattern of buying and selling, and ultimately to a successful business enterprise. ■ Once in Engelstad's employ, Clyne spearheaded many a dramatic effort to obtain cars for the Collection, among them the purchase of Hollywood's venerable Pacific Auto Rental, a deal that involved obtaining the entire company and its stable of 128 cars, just to get to one automobile—the extremely rare 1938 Mercedes-Benz G4 Geländewagen. ■ Another venture led Clyne to the doorsteps of W. C. Fields' mistress, actress Carlotta Monti, who, following the famous comedian's death in

■ At the bottom of the page, far left, one of the Collection's craftsmen takes the rough edges off one fender, while in the picture to the right, a second craftsman wet sands another prior to painting in order to eliminate any imperfections. At the top of the page is an assortment of restored gauges and lights; to the right, a still-life is composed from spare Mercedes-Benz radiator shells. A warehouse alongside the Collection's restoration shop holds thousands of parts—everything from hood ornaments to complete engines.

■ The Imperial Palace functions as host to "The Auction," an annual event run jointly by

Richie Clyne and Don Williams, administrators of, respectively, the Imperial Palace and the Behring Museum of Blackhawk,

California. Originally organized to facilitate the sale of surplus cars from the two museums, the event

soon attracted sellers—as well as buyers—from all across the country and around the world. The special allure

of the annual event is its "no reserve" policy, which assures the sale of every entry.

1949, was left with nothing but his 1938 Cadillac V-16—a treasure she had sentimentally maintained in a small garage behind her rented apartment. Repeated wooing by Clyne could not convince Monti to part with the car, until Clyne finally worked out a package deal that included the promise that mannequins of Fields and Monti would be displayed with the car. ■ In recent years the Collection has changed direction once again as the targets for acquisition have become the absolute cream of the automotive crop—today, it encompasses one of the world's largest concentrations of Duesenbergs, American Rolls-Royces and late-Thirties Mercedes-Benzes. Many of these treasured examples of automotive history have been painstakingly resurrected in the Collection's own fully equipped, 25,000-square-foot restoration facility which includes individual departments devoted to paint, bodywork, upholstery repair and mechanical restoration. ■ One of the world's ten best automotive museums, the Imperial Palace Auto Collection now features over 600 cars and continues to grow as the selection is refined and expanded. With the passing of nearly three million visitors down its aisles to date, the Collection is also one of the world's most popular, and, as such, stands as a tribute to the man whose dream it represents, but more profoundly, as a monument to the creative passions that gave the world the automobile.

■ *Billed as "The Sale of the Century," the two-day event indeed lives up to its appellation.*

Limited to 500 automobiles, The Auction is attended by some 3000 registered bidders, arriving from such far corners of

the world as Hong Kong and Johannesburg. The elite automobiles that have passed across the block

at record-breaking prices include one of the six Bugatti Royales—its unforgettable visage seen in the picture at

the bottom left—which reached the $11,000,000 mark in the 1989 auction.

PART TWO

THE DETAILS

■ The following ten pages focus on the details that make up the whole of an automobile
—elements that present both visual beauty and technical interest. Displayed on this page are the faces of some of the
most unique and trendsetting automobiles ever created. Below, the novel horseshoe shape of the Bugatti
radiator has been its trademark since Ettore Bugatti began building cars in 1909. Here, the radiator of a 1937 Type 57
reflects subtle design changes introduced by Ettore's talented son, Jean.

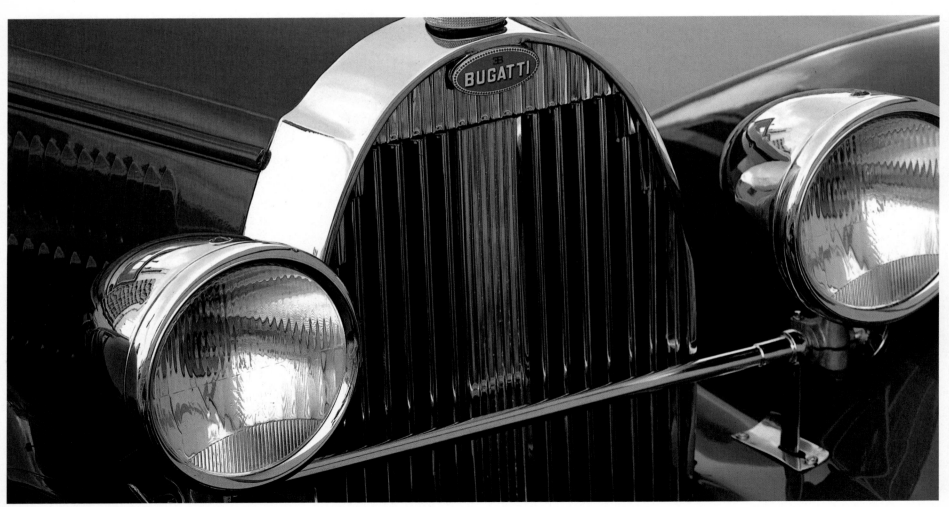

■ Four masterpieces of the art of steel sculpture are represented in the illustrations on this page.

Top left, the 1948 Tucker by Alex Tremulis. Next to it, Gordon Buehrig's 1937 Cord 812, whose retractable headlights

were an automotive first and an essential part of the look that made this Cord one of the all-time styling

greats. At the bottom of the page, Phil Wright's 1933 Pierce-Arrow Silver Arrow. To the right, the curvaceous

extravagance of Harley Earl, as expressed by the 1957 Cadillac.

■ Speed and flight were among the favorite themes of many classic hood ornaments.

At the top of this page is Buick's Mercury, cast in a variety of configurations by Ternstedt of Detroit. Below it, Packard's "Goddess of Speed" took its cue from a similar design Bazin created for Isotta Fraschini. To the right, the "Spirit of the Wind" decorates a 1939 Packard radiator. This design was created by Réné Lalique, France's famous glass and jewelry maker, and can be illuminated by a bulb located in its base.

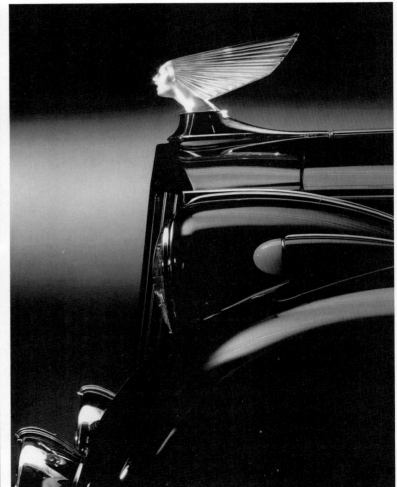

■ Rolls-Royce's "Spirit of Ecstasy" came in a variety of sizes and metals. At first fitted sporadically, the mascot became a catalog item in 1921. In the early days, sculptor Sykes put the finishing touches to each copy, giving them a special individuality. The metals he specified corresponded roughly to the ones used in the radiators themselves, polished bronze when radiators were made from bronze, nickel-plating in the days of nickel, and chrome-plating when radiators were built from stainless steel.

■ *This photograph of the dashboard from the Collection's 1916 Simplex highlights the exquisite craftsmanship that characterized the era in general and this car in particular. Its nautical theme, notable in a number of exterior details, was carried through to the interior, where a smoothly crafted railing curves around the entire cockpit. Having been cosseted by connoisseurs all its life—as indicated by its 1947 Glidden Tour badge—the Simplex is completely original, down to its eight-day Waltham clock.*

■ At right, the instruments from the Collection's 1933 Pierce-Arrow Silver Arrow are tastefully but logically grouped in a tight cluster. At the bottom of the page, the speedometer and clock mounted in the rear compartment of a 1931 Cadillac V-16 dual-cowl phaeton kept passengers informed of time and motion. Pictured to the left are the steering wheel and instrument cluster of the 1948 Tucker, which, in keeping with its advanced design theme, were a radical departure from the designs of the classic era.

■ *An even dozen was the perfect number of wooden spokes on Renault's 1923 artillery-type wheel, seen in the illustration below. The hub carried no decoration—just a simple "Automobiles Renault" spelled out in a circle. By 1939, spoked wheels, both wood and metal, had been supplemented by pressed-steel wheels topped by hubcaps as seen below, right, on a Cadillac V-16. Its super-wide white sidewalls provide a commanding yet delicate counterpoint for the V-16 logo at the center of the wheel.*

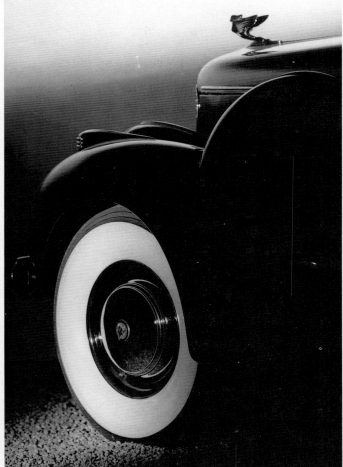

■ *Fifty-six tempered steel spokes support the hub of this Rolls-Royce wheel. The automobile shown in this photograph is a 1928 Springfield model, built in the Massachusetts town of the same name. Its wheels were manufactured by the Wire Wheel Corporation of America, located in Buffalo, New York, and were distinctive because of the recessed center portion of the hub nut. A special tool, supplied as one of the twenty-seven items in the tool box, fit the shape of this recess and permitted removal of the wheel.*

■ The engine compartment of a 1947 Delahaye is accessible through an exquisitely

shaped hood, its twin lids opening like wings. In the picture below, left, the long valve cover of its straight six is topped by

a parallel row of brightly polished carburetors, a combination that suggests a powerful elegance.

The engine compartment of a 1916 Simplex, right, surrounds a well-orchestrated display of iron, brass and copper.

At the bottom of the page is a close-up of the heart of a 1915 Rolls-Royce Silver Ghost.

■ Seen here is one of the most outstanding engines of all time, the supercharged

Duesenberg SJ. This is not the standard 320-hp version, however, but one fitted with the "rams-horn" intake manifold

that breathed through two carburetors—in contrast to the standard SJ supercharger, which used

only one. Said to increase engine output from 320 hp to as much as 400, the system was initially developed

for the "Duesenberg Special" Land Speed Record car but was later installed on a handful of SJs.

PART THREE

THE AUTOMOBILES

LA NEF

THREE-WHEELER

■ The three-wheeler has been around since the earliest days of self-propelled vehicles. In fact, the first such vehicle to move successfully under its own power is thought to have been the 1771 steam-engined gun carriage built by Frenchman Nicolas Cugnot, the humble son of a farmer whose crude design featured two wheels at the rear and one up front. ■ The ease with which the steering function could be engineered seems to have been a deciding factor behind several pioneers' choice of the three-wheel layout. This was certainly the case when Carl Benz built his first self-propelled vehicle in 1886—the progenitor of the modern automobile. ■ The same system was also chosen by French pioneers Albert de Dion and Georges Bouton, who in 1895 fitted a gasoline engine of their own design to a three-wheeler. Engines of De Dion-Bouton manufacture were ultimately used in a large number of automobiles worldwide—160 by 1914. Among these were many famous names, such as Sunbeam and Humber in Great Britain and Pierce-Arrow and Peerless in the United States. ■ An obscure and virtually forgotten customer of the De Dion-Bouton powerplant was a Frenchman named La Croix, an eccentric inventor and sometime photographer who, in 1899, established the firm of La Croix de Laville in Agen, France. Its purpose was to facilitate manufacture of a vehicle based on a prototype he had built that year—a curious

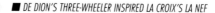

three-wheeler. ■ La Croix placed the one-cylinder, 8-hp engine up front in a wooden frame whose two longitudinal members curved inwards as well as upwards, coming to a point above the single front wheel. Steering was controlled through a tiller, which, with a length of 63 inches, must have been something of a record. The wheelbase measured 86 inches. ■ Power was transmitted through a Bozier gearbox to the right-rear wheel via belt drive. The driver, who occupied the left side of the vehicle and steered with his right hand, could affect road speed in two ways—by regulating the throttle or by adjusting the tension of the belt; controls for both of which were located on the left-hand side. The brakes, acting on the rear wheels only, were operated via a foot pedal. Topping off this eccentric piece of machinery was a four-place body with the two rear seats accessible only from the rear. Top speed is not known, but prudence should have kept it low. ■ The La Nef—a fancy French word for ship—probably atttracted more smiles than admiration: Imagine the driver attempting to negotiate a sharp turn, a maneuver that would have required either leaning outside the car in a dramatic fashion or sliding across to the other side of the seat. The fact that the peculiar vehicle was still available as late as 1914—by which time some 200 had been built—can only be attributed to the endearing quality of French humor.

DAIMLER

MODEL 45 CONVERTIBLE SALOON

■ Daimler stands for distinction in more ways than one. Not only can the lineage of this British stalwart be traced back to the birth of the automobile, it can also count a royal connection like no other.

■ In 1888, two years after Gottlieb Daimler's first automobile appeared on the dusty roads of Cannstatt, Germany, Englishman Frederick Simms arranged a meeting with the inventor. Duly impressed, he acquired the British rights to Daimler's engines. In 1893, Simms formed the Daimler Motor Syndicate, only to sell it three years later. The new owners invited Gottlieb Daimler to become a member of the board, a post he held for two years, by which time the first all-British Daimler had been built. ■ The connection with the Crown commenced virtually the moment the Daimler appeared; in 1898, the Prince of Wales was treated to his first demonstration tour over open roads. Two years later, seven months before the death of Queen Victoria, the Prince ordered three Daimlers. Upon ascending the throne to become King Edward VII, his Daimlers ascended with him, becoming the first to inhabit the royal garage. It was an association that would continue unbroken for more than half a century. ■ By the outbreak of World War I, Daimler had compiled a track record of incredible variation. The firm had produced engines with displacements stretching from less than one liter to more than ten, in configurations ranging from simple side-valve twins to sixes sporting the complex sleeve-valve system adopted in 1909. The types of vehicles produced were no less varied; in addition to the grand royal coaches, there was an array of stately touring machines, as well as, at the opposite end of the spectrum, buses and other commercial vehicles. ■ The post-war years began with a limited selection. One of the two types offered was the Model 45, of which the Collection's Windover-bodied example is a typical illustration—although with a twist. This exquisite automobile was ordered by the Maharajah of Alewar, whose marital arrangement necessitated frequent countryside outings, occasions requiring a certain amount of privacy—this, it is alleged, explains the presence of the finely crafted wooden blinds.

■ The Model 45's six-cylinder sleeve-valve engine has a bore and stroke of 110 mm by 130, a displacement of 7.4 liters (452 cubic inches) and an output of 65 hp at 1400 rpm. Its wheelbase is an impressive 146 inches. Daimler went on to build a pair of progressive overhead-valve V-8s, as well as a massive V-12—mastodons powering some of the most elephantine expressions of the coachbuilder's craft. ■ A unifying element distinguishing all Daimler cars since 1904 has been their fluted radiator shell. Although Daimler was absorbed by Jaguar in 1960, this trademark of tradition still graces the models produced by its new owners.

CORD

MODEL L-29 CABRIOLET

■ To imagine the era of the great classics without Auburn, Cord and Duesenberg is to imagine the films of the Thirties without Garbo, Gable and Harlow; in either case, much of the glamour would be gone. ■ The power behind these magnificent cars was generated almost entirely by one man: Errett Lobban Cord. In 1924, Cord, only thirty years old, had taken over management of stagnating Auburn. Sales soared immediately, energized primarily by cosmetic changes. ■ By 1929, Cord had gained control of the company. Flush with success, he went after Duesenberg. The firm had fallen on hard times and lacked the capital to develop a new model. Soon Cord's injection of cash and his inspiring vision brought forth the legendary Model J. ■ But there was more to come. Cord needed a product to fill the gap between the low-end Auburn and the high-end Duesenberg. It would have front-wheel drive. And it would carry the Cord name. That the Indianapolis successes of Harry Miller's front-wheel-drive racers had influenced Cord became obvious when he bought the patent rights in 1927. Cord soon assembled an engineering team and sent it to work at Miller's Los Angeles shop. ■ By the end of 1928, the action had moved to Indianapolis; the chassis was ready to receive a body, and Auburn designer John Oswald proved the man for the task. The result was the most striking automobile of its day. Measuring just 50 inches from the road to the top of its hood, the machine stood ten inches lower than the competition. ■ Contributing further to its rakish look was the long sweep of the hood, a feature necessitated by the length of the engine, which had been turned back to front, locating the transmission ahead of the block. The hood could have been even longer; the engine penetrated six inches into the driver's compartment. ■ The L-29's side-valve, straight-eight power source, built by Lycoming—a company also owned by Cord— had a bore and stroke of 3.3 inches by 4.5, a displacement of 299 cubic inches (4.9 liters) and an output of 115 hp at 3300 rpm. The three-speed, non-synchromesh transmission was operated via a dashboard-mounted handle. Top speed of the 137.5-inch wheel-base, 4620-pound package was less than 80 mph—making its allure not so much a matter of being fast, but looking fast. ■ Sales met with resistance, but this was less the result of problems related to front-wheel drive than it was directly connected with the Crash—coming only three months after the L-29's introduction. The original price of $3295—for the Cabriolet—was soon lowered to $2495. . . in vain. By the middle of 1932, after 4429 had been built, the conveyor of the Cord name was put to rest—but not permanently. A few years hence the appellation would be resurrected for yet another masterpiece—the Cord 810.

MERCEDES

MODEL 8/18 TOWN CAR

■ *During the first decade of the twentieth century, Daimler and Benz—who would join forces as Daimler-Benz in 1926—still functioned separately, both pursuing the perfection of their individual products. Daimler was the more prominent of the two, however, as the Cannstatt firm possessed the brilliant engineering talent of Wilhelm Maybach and Paul Daimler. Yet it is unlikely that the road to success would have run so straight had it not been for Emil Jellinek, a colorful entrepreneur whose playground was Nice on the French Riviera.* ■ *Having placed an order for four cars with Daimler in 1896, Jellinek soon bought six more, which put him in a position to make constructive suggestions about the product, such as moving the engine from the middle to the front, enlarging it from two to four cylinders in the process—the automobile would never be the same.* ■ *In 1890, with the cars duly revised, Jellinek entered one of them in the Nice-La Turbie hillclimb. The result was not glory but disaster, with a crash killing the driver. Undaunted, Jellinek blamed the car and suggested further improvements, backing his request with a third order—this time for thirty-six. He also demanded that the new model be named Mercedes, after one of his daughters.* ■ *The Mercedes was a sensation; the 1901 Nice Week, which incorporated a long distance race, a sprint and a hillclimb, saw the newcomer win all three events. Followed*

by many more victories, this coup helped to form a foundation for commercial success. ■ Among those watching the events from this side of the Atlantic was multi-millionaire William Kissam Vanderbilt. Having purchased one of the earliest Mercedes cars in 1901, he three years later took delivery of another—a powerful Type 90 racer—and proceeded to Ormond Beach, Florida, where he covered the flying mile at a speed of 92 mph, traveling faster than any man before him. Again, racing generated sales and Mercedes became the best-selling imported car in America. ■ Another Mercedes enthusiast and multi-millionaire was John Jacob Astor, whose fortune rested on Manhattan real estate. One of the cars in his Mercedes stable has survived and is featured here, an exquisite town car bodied by Belvallette of Paris. Built in 1909—the year in which the three-pointed star first appeared on the radiator—it remains in original condition, its luxurious cloth interior giving off the unmistakable scent of history. In contrast to its imposing dimensions, its four-cylinder engine produced a moderate 18 hp at 1200 rpm. ■ John Jacob Astor went down with the Titanic on that fateful night in 1912. His Mercedes remained in the family, stored for more than four decades in a Bronx warehouse. Later, the heirs moved the car to the family estate in Florida, from where it was brought to the Collection.

CADILLAC

MODEL 452A DUAL-COWL PHAETON

■ As the Roaring Twenties churned inexorably towards a tumultuous climax, an ever-escalating stock market made millionaires out of common people. Flappers and movie stars, bootleggers and gangsters all became symbols of an era that knew no limits. ■ The luxury automobile flourished in this climate. Yet the golden age of coachbuilding demanded larger, more powerful engines to carry heavier, more elaborate bodies. With conventional straight-eights stretched to their rough-running limits, smoothness became the catchword. The move towards the ultimate machine, the sixteen, had begun. ■ It fell to Larry Fisher, new head of Cadillac in 1925, and his man in charge of engine development, Owen Nacker, to create the first American V-16. In Europe, Ettore Bugatti had conceived a sixteen-cylinder aircraft engine in 1917. The U.S. Government was interested, and the man sent to investigate, Howard Marmon—who would introduce his own sixteen in 1931— gave the thumbs up. Duesenberg was awarded the contract, but by the time the engine stood ready to enter production, the war was over and only eleven units resulted. ■ Marmon and Nacker were good friends; when Fisher called, Nacker had already given much thought to a V-16. Its final design placed the cylinders in a 45-degree vee. Bore and stroke measured 3.0 inches by 4.0, producing a displacement of 7.4 liters, or 452 cubic inches—the source, as

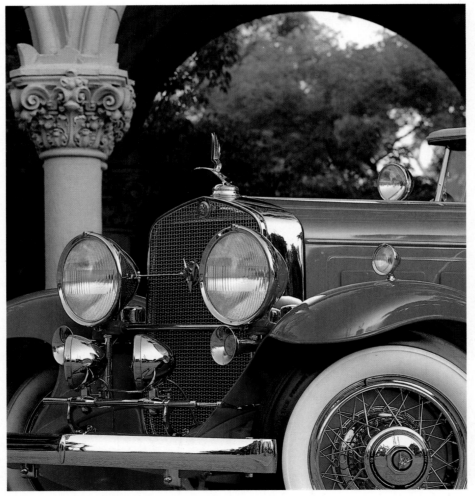

was the Cadillac style, of its official designation. Two overhead valves per cylinder were operated through pushrods and rockers, commanded by a camshaft located in the center of the vee. Output was 165 hp at 3400 rpm. With a weight of around 6000 pounds, the 148-inch-wheelbase, three-speed-transmission package managed about 90 mph. ■ Cadillac's goal for the Sixteen, however, was not so much performance as it was prestige—a commodity partly attributable to Harley Earl's styling. His inspiration came from Europe and the Hispano-Suiza. But it was not merely a matter of transference—Earl's talent was too great. From the huge headlamps, to the smooth fenderline, to the upturned rear—it was all Earl, all elegance. ■ By the time the Sixteen faced the public in January 1930, Wall Street's darkest hour still cast its doomsday shadows. But work continued in the Fleetwood facilities and by June 1930, 2000 cars had been built. The last half of the year saw another 887. The following year added a final 364. The Collection's example carried a price tag of $6500, and represents one of only 85 Fleetwood-bodied phaetons. ■ Unlike many of its peers, Cadillac survived the Crash. Its V-16 went on to power a succession of restyled models, staying in production until 1937, when a new, less complex version carried the torch for three more years. That, as they say, was the end of an era.

H O R C H

TYP 670 SPORT CABRIOLET

■ August Horch, born in 1868, looms large in the annals of German auto manufacture. His influence embraces not only the firm that made his name famous, established in 1899, but also another important marque, Audi, founded a decade later. ■ The record of Horch's early career illustrates the tightly woven world of the pioneers. His first experience came during a three-year stint as an engineer in the employ of Carl Benz. After Horch had been forced out of the firm bearing his name in 1900, Paul Daimler—the son of fellow pioneer Gottlieb Daimler—became its chief engineer. Another thread leads to Fritz Fiedler, who headed Horch's ambitious V-12 project in the early Thirties before going on to further fame in the halls of BMW, where he engineered such immortal sporting machines as the 328 and the 507. ■ In the mid-Twenties, Horch had been the first in Germany to feature straight-eight power. This had been a period of confidence, but a few years later, on the threshold of a new decade, Horch's management suffered from disillusionment after its product was eclipsed by Mercedes-Benz's fabulous flagship, the 770K, and Maybach's magnificent engineering triumph, the Zeppelin. The decision was made to try to outmaneuver the rivals with a V-12-powered mastadon, the Type 600, a long-wheelbase, limousine-style automobile first exhibited at the Paris Salon in the fall of 1931. ■ But while the product was well

thought out, the timing was not, and only twenty 600s were built. The V-12 engine also found its way into the Type 670, which rested on a shorter, 125-inch wheelbase. Produced between 1931 and 1934, the 670—of which just 58 were built—was available in two open versions. ■ Fiedler's 60-degree, single-overhead-cam V-12 sported a bore and stroke of 80 mm by 100, a displacement of an even 6.0 liters (368 cubic inches) and an output of 120 hp at 3200 rpm, which gave the 5390-pound five-seater a top speed of 85 mph. The four-speed transmission featured a world first: synchromesh in all four gears. ■ The 670 shown here carries the characteristic windshield with angled corner windows, drawn by Horch's own Hermann Ahrens and built by the Glachau-based firm of Dietzsch. One of only three known survivors, the rare machine was added to the Collection in 1987 after having been purchased at that year's Sotheby Auction in Geneva. ■ In 1933, August Horch made a triumphant return to the organization he had left twenty-four years earlier. During the next few years, he led the Zwickau-based firm into a period of final greatness. The outbreak of war, however, put a halt to automobile production, and the emphasis shifted to the manufacture of troop carriers. No cars were built after the war, and August Horch retired to a small town in Bavaria, where he died in 1951.

■ HORCH'S OWN SPEZIAL-ROADSTER RIVALED MERCEDES

ROLLS-ROYCE

PHANTOM I TRANSFORMABLE

■ A shop on Taylor Street in Springfield, Massachusetts, was the 1895 birthplace of the earliest series-built American automobile, the Duryea. This machine proved of such interest to the British that production was organized in England in 1902. ■ Two decades later, in a reverse parallel, Rolls-Royce decided to set up shop in America, settling in, of all places, Springfield. The selection was made because the city—a site of both rifle and motorcycle factories—boasted a highly skilled labor force. It was, in fact, a former Indian Motorcycle plant that in 1920 became the home of Rolls-Royce of America, Inc. ■ Due to a wave of postwar demand, British Rolls faced a two-year backlog of orders, a problem an American factory would help alleviate. British law prohibited transfer of assets, however, so the American firm was financed by domestic interests. Managers and foremen, on the other hand, were brought over from the Rolls works in Derby. This was done to prevent two sets of standards—a Rolls had to be a Rolls no matter where it was built. ■ That this goal had been met became evident when the first American chassis appeared in 1921; despite the fact that the entire car had been assembled on this side of the Atlantic, the American copy was identical to the original. ■ But when Rolls-Royce of America bought the Brewster coachbuilding firm in 1925—and began to supply complete cars—the character of the

Springfield issue changed considerably, not in quality, but in style. Brewster produced a catalog that listed no less than twenty-eight bodies, which all, appropriately, were named after English towns—such as Oxford, Pickwick and Wimbledon. ■ Mechanically, the Springfield Rolls shared its specifications with the Derby version, the Phantom I engine being an inline six, with a bore and stroke of 108 mm by 140, a displacement of 7.7 liters (470 cubic inches) and an output of 80 hp at 2250 rpm. There were two wheelbase choices available—143.5 inches and 146.5. With 1924 prices for bodied cars ranging from $12,930 to $15,880, the Rolls was America's most expensive car. ■ When the Phantom II arrived in 1929, Springfield could not afford to retool. Imported chassis, mixed with outdated domestic ones, kept the company going until 1934, by which time 2944 cars had been built. ■ The Collection's example features a body by Hibbard & Darrin, the famous Paris-based firm headed by two American expatriates. This created the awkward combination of an American-built chassis being shipped to France—with England just across the channel—then, after application of the coachwork, being shipped back to America. But these were times when the selection of a new automobile was never taken lightly; as with choosing a future bride, the decision was intended to be of lasting duration.

PIERCE-ARROW

SILVER ARROW

■ In the early Thirties, it was widely believed that the time for streamlined automobiles had come. It was thought that soon, perhaps within a decade, all cars would look like teardrops. ■ The earliest impulses came from Europe, where Swiss scientist Paul Jaray—constructing bizarre cars that excelled in theoretical accuracy but lacked artistic flair—had become something of a guru. In America, interest was spurred by the experiments of aircraft pioneer Glenn Curtiss, who in 1928 performed wind-tunnel tests with conventional cars. ■ The auto industry watched with interest, but moved cautiously. Then, in 1932, former GM stylist Phil Wright approached Pierce-Arrow with a proposal for a sweepingly futuristic design. ■ At the time it was common knowledge that Pierce-Arrow was on the ropes. Four years earlier, it had been forced to accept a merger with Studebaker, but the downward drift had continued and by 1932 production had sunk to 2692 units. Management was desperate. In October, they accepted Wright's proposal. ■ Only five units were to be built—in secrecy, and in a hurry. The needed chassis were immediately shipped from Buffalo to South Bend, where the Studebaker engineering department gathered a team of three dozen craftsmen. Chief body engineer James Hughes, given a deadline only three months away, was placed in charge. Working around the clock, the seemingly impossible task

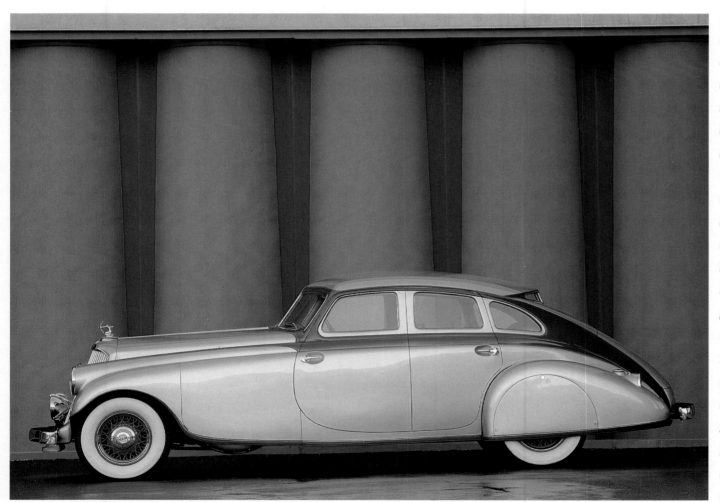

was accomplished on time. ■ When Wright, who had been cut out of the process, saw the finished product, he realized his original design had been tampered with. Hughes had exchanged the original rear end for one from a Studebaker show car that included a small, vee-shaped window. Further reason for the altered design lay with the contraction required by a change to a 139-inch wheelbase from the 147-inch length originally specified. Otherwise, Wright's shape was intact, with faired-in headlights, flowing pontoon-like front fenders carrying concealed spare wheels and teardrop-shaped rear fenders with full-length skirts. ■ Power came from Pierce-Arrow's L-head V-12, featuring a bore and stroke of 3.5 inches by 4.0, a displacement of 462 cubic inches (7.6 liters) and an output of 175 hp at 3400 rpm. The unit propelled the 5729-pound car to a top speed of 115 mph. The transmission was a three-speed gearbox equipped with a free-wheeling device. ■ The Silver Arrow owned by the Collection was shipped to Buffalo on February 11, 1933. It still stands as it did back then, untouched, except for its paint. The first Silver Arrow was sent to the New York Auto Show, where it caused a sensation. Although a show stopper, it failed to save the company. Probably nothing, short of a miracle, could have done that. But the Silver Arrow was as close to a miracle as anyone could have come.

DUESENBERG

MODEL SJ DUAL-COWL PHAETON

■ *In spite of the fame of the Duesenberg race car—the first and only American machine to have won the French Grand Prix—its companion road car, as marketed during most of the Twenties, failed to generate the excitement produced by its competition counterpart.* ■ *This was partly a result of its coachwork, which took its cue from men whose minds were crowded by issues of engineering and failed to match the effervescence of the machinery. It was with the 1926 arrival of E. L. Cord, and his inspiring dream of creating an automobile on a grand scale, that the Duesenberg reached its zenith.* ■ *The emergence of Duesenberg as "The World's Finest Motor Car" could not have happened without the engineering genius of Fred Duesenberg. It is equally clear that the feat would never have been accomplished without the financial backing and inspired guidance of Cord. Likewise, without Gordon Buehrig—the designer who, at age twenty-five, became responsible for the Duesenberg look—the circles combining form and function would never have been so perfectly joined.* ■ *The man whose prolific pen would give shape to more than half of all Duesenbergs produced went from high school in Peoria, Illinois, through courses in drafting, art and metal shop at Bradley College, to an apprenticeship at the Gotfredson Body Company in Wayne, Michigan. Further turns on the road to Duesenberg were negoti-*

ated at Packard, General Motors and Stutz. ■ Harold Ames, Duesenberg's sales manager, was responsible for hiring Buehrig. Ames was also the man who, together with Cord and Auburn designer Al Leamy, established the shape that defined the Duesenberg look, such as the radiator shell, the hood and the fenders. Only the mascot was Buehrig's creation. ■ The lines of the La Grande dual-cowl phaeton represented here became something of a Duesenberg trademark with its characteristic "sweep panel" that flowed from the hood down across the front doors. Buehrig's inspiration for the La Grande came from a design created by Le Baron, but it was Buehrig's genius that elevated the shape to its level of artistic perfection. ■ The builder, the Union City Body Company of Union City, Indiana, was not a prestige carriage house. In a classic example of salesmanship, Ames invented the La Grande name, adding a touch of acquired class. Delivered to Duesenberg's Indianapolis facility in the white, the bodies were finished by in-house craftsmen. The chassis demanded a stately $8500, with the body adding $4000 to $6500. ■ The Duesenberg shown here first carried a sedate sedan body. Later, when more power and flashier coachwork was desired, the engine received a supercharger and the chassis a La Grande-style body, one that in its superb execution emulates all the grace and beauty of the original.

STUTZ

MODEL DV-32 VICTORIA

■ Stutz holds a special place among American classics, one earned not only through its advanced engineering and its racing successes, but also through its image, which was burnished with a certain European flair. ■ Born in 1876 on an Ohio farm, Harry Clayton Stutz soon left the rural ways of his Dutch parents for bustling Dayton. Years filled with a variety of ventures followed, but by 1910 he had moved on to Indianapolis, where he built a potent racer. Entered in the 1911 inaugural of the 500-mile race, the Stutz finished in eleventh place—not bad for a debutant. ■ When Stutz began building replicas of his Indianapolis car, its racing roots were recalled with the famous slogan "The Car That Made Good in a Day." In another linguistic coup, Stutz called his roadster "Bearcat"—a catchy name for a hairy machine of true sports car heritage. ■ The company initiated public trading of its stock in 1915, a venture that drove Harry Stutz out of the firm in 1919 when manipulator Alan Ryan bought control of the company, culminating in a debacle remembered on Wall Street as the "Stutz Corner." Harry Stutz went on to fame as a builder of fire trucks, but died prematurely in 1930. ■ The Twenties saw Stutz adrift—a tack broken by the arrival of Frederick Moskovics, the Hungarian emigré of Marmon fame, who charted a new course by charging Charles Greuter, a Swiss-born engineer, with the task of creating an

eight-cylinder engine that would emulate the single-overhead-cam tradition of Europe's famed Alfas and Hispanos. Wrapped in an ever-increasing variety of coachwork—twenty-eight bodystyles were offered in 1928—the Vertical Eight brought both sales—a record production of 5000 in 1926—and racing successes—a sensational second at Le Mans in 1928. ■ By 1931, the multi-cylinder war forced Stutz, whose Depression-ravaged coffers could not afford a new engine, to creative exploitation of its existing straight-eight. The DV-32—named for its valvetrain—sounded aggressively advanced, even superior, when compared to the competition's V-12s and V-16s. Sporting double overhead cams and hemispherical combustion chambers, the DV-32's bore and stroke of 3.4 inches by 4.5 created a displacement of 322 cubic inches (5.2 liters) and an output of 156 hp at 3900 rpm. Mounted in the Bearcat—a name revived for a shorter, 135-inch-wheelbase model—the engine produced a top speed of over 100 mph. ■ The Collection's DV-32—its 145-inch chassis supporting an exquisite Rollston body costing $7400—spent its postwar years under a bridge in the Bronx, parked there by a GI who never returned. ■ Despite Stutz's avant-garde image, production, by 1933, had dwindled to 110 units. The following year, with only six cars assembled, marked the final demise of once-proud Stutz.

■ THE BEARCAT GAVE STUTZ A BIG-NAME SPORTS CAR

HISPANO-SUIZA

TYPE J12 TRANSFORMABLE

■ The name Hispano-Suiza refers to Spain, where the marque originated, and to Switzerland, the birthplace of Marc Birkigt, whose engineering brilliance guided Hispano from the beginning to the end. ■ Birkigt's offspring earned a reputation as a first among equals, an epithet stemming not only from their remarkable engineering but also from the bodies created for them by the world's finest coachbuilders—an amalgam of the best of both disciplines. ■ Hispano referred to its product as "The Queen of Automobiles." It might have been more appropriate, however, to have adopted the appellation of "King"—Spain's Alfonso XIII acquired a Hispano in 1905 and later allowed a model to carry his name. ■ The roots of the Alfonso were found in a racer that won France's "Coup de l'Auto" in 1910. The success created a demand among French buyers and a subsidiary was set up in Paris. The factory at first occupied an old tram depot alongside the Seine in Levallois-Perret, but was later moved to a facility in Bois-Colombes, from which all of the classic Hispanos originated. ■ During World War I, Hispano's manufacturing emphasis switched to aircraft engines, an involvement inspiring the most famous of the Hispano automobiles, the H6, with its fabulous overhead-cam, six-cylinder power plant. ■ The climax—some say the anti-climax—was reached in 1931 with the V-12 powered J12. Its complex pushrod-

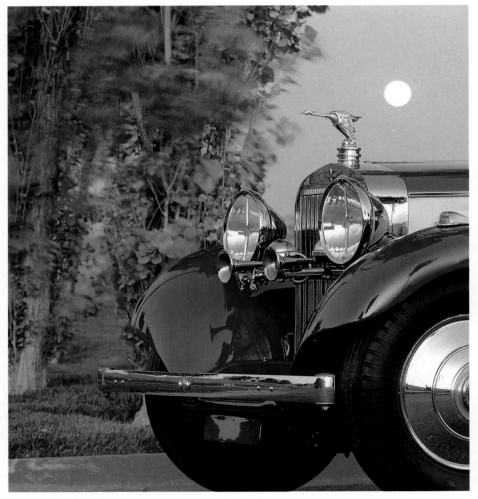

activated valvetrain exchanged the H6's mechanical sophistication for a less exotic but quieter design. Bore and stroke were an even 100 mm by 100, displacement 9.4 liters (575 cubic inches) and output 220 hp at 3000 rpm. ■ The J12 continued the use of Birkigt's legendary servo-assisted brakes, but the three-speed gearbox, with its too-high first gear and the less-than-adequate multiplate clutch, were no match for the 5000-pound giant. Once the initial inertia was overcome, however, the J12 ate up the road— 0 to 60 mph took just 12 seconds. Top speed was around 100 mph. ■ No less than four wheelbases were available, the longest measuring 158 inches. Only 120 J12s had been built when Birkigt put aside automobiles in 1938 to concentrate, once again, on aircraft engines. The Hispano-Suiza badge was never again to grace an automobile. With a postwar world completely changed, Birkigt retired to Switzerland, where he died in 1953. ■ The Collection's J12 features a one-off body by Saoutchik, the prestigious Parisian coachbuilder. Commissioned by a British gentleman named Batcock, its sumptuous passenger compartment boasts a finely crafted cabinet, complete with decanters and glasses as well as a comb and mirror on the ladies side, and cigar box and cutter on the gentleman's side—trappings befitting an automobile that so perfectly reflected the aspirations of the upper crust.

■ THIS ARTIST'S DREAM WAS A REALITY OF THE RICH

MERCEDES-BENZ

TYP 500K SPEZIAL-ROADSTER

■ The past glory of Mercedes-Benz should weigh heavily on present-day management as it looks back on the fabulous machines the firm created in the Twenties and Thirties. Perhaps it is no coincidence that the company's once common practice of including classics in its advertising seems to have been abandoned. The exclusivity of the handcrafted automobiles, matched by the beauty of their lines, no longer provide flattering comparisons with products from the age of robot technology. ■ It was the 1926 amalgamation of Daimler and Benz that spawned a special breed of Mercedes-Benz sports car. Those were the days of the Ferdinand Porsche-designed SSKs and SSKLs, muscular monsters powered by huge supercharged sixes that swept clean the racing circuits, rip-roaring and tail-spinning their way to immortality. ■ After a period of financial difficulties during the Depression, the early Thirties saw Mercedes-Benz return with vigor. The German economy bustled from the energy of a new political system, one of whose grand projects was the construction of the Autobahn highway network. This challenged Mercedes-Benz to design an automobile capable of sustained high-speed driving. The new breed should not be seen as a sports car in the past sense, but as a machine combining power and elegance as never before. ■ Porsche had left Daimler-Benz in 1928; his place had been taken by Hans Nibel, a veteran from the days of the 1908 Grand Prix Benz. The first of Nibel's designs, introduced in 1933 as the 380, was powered by a 3.8-liter, overhead-valve, straight eight. Found low on power, its displacement was increased to 5.0 liters (306 cubic inches) in 1934, and the model designation changed to 500K—the K denoting the addition of a "Kompressor," or supercharger. ■ The Collection's 500K represents a design first seen at the 1935 Berlin Auto Show. The Spezial-Roadster was the sportiest among a choice of nine bodystyles—drawn by Hermann Ahrens and built by the Stuttgart firm's own Sindelfingen coachworks. Records indicate that only twenty-nine Spezial-Roadsters were produced, a figure that includes an unspecified number of Normal-Roadsters—identified by their flat windscreens.

■ The Spezial-Roadster rests on a 119-inch wheelbase, weighs 4775 pounds, has a four-speed gearbox, servo-assisted hydraulic brakes and fully independent suspension. Bore and stroke are 86 mm by 108, output 100 hp at 3400 rpm—160 hp with the supercharger engaged. ■ A sixteen-second burst jettisons the machine to 60 mph. Another rush brings on the top speed of nearly 100 mph, a figure the driver—if he is able to break the spell of the screaming supercharger—can confirm with a glance at the speedometer, which, as befits this contradiction of elegance and power, is set in a glamorous mother-of-pearl dash.

DUESENBERG

MODEL J TOWN CAR

■ In 1878, in the town of Lippe, Germany, the Duesenbergs welcomed a new addition to their family—a son, christened Frederic. A year later, another son arrived; he would be called August. Seven years later, inspired by glowing reports from the New World, the family emigrated to America. ■ By the time they reached their nineteenth and twentieth birthdays, the Duesenberg brothers had distinguished themselves by building and racing bicycles. In 1898, for example, Fred set a world record over the two-mile distance. It was only natural that the brothers would choose to manufacture bicycles of their own, but their first venture, established in Des Moines, succumbed to bankruptcy in 1903. ■ The brothers remained in Des Moines, and it was here, in 1904, that they built their first automobile, the robust and racy two-cylinder Mason. It took another few years before they reached the Brickyard, but their improved four-cylinder Mason failed to qualify. ■ A decade later, the picture was dramatically different. In 1913, the Duesenbergs founded their own firm, and in 1921, Jimmy Murphy drove a straight-eight Duesenberg to victory in the French Grand Prix. The Duesenberg went on to become one of the most famous racing machines of the era, winning the Indianapolis 500 in 1924, 1925 and 1927. ■ A road car, the Model A, had been introduced in 1920, but its drowsy bodywork made it a slow seller, and by

1927 the brothers were once again in trouble—only to be saved by E. L. Cord. ■ The Cord era brought Duesenberg into the company of the world's greatest cars thanks to the engineering genius of Fred Duesenberg, the styling talent of Gordon Buehrig and the financial savvy of Errett Lobban Cord. ■ The crown jewel of the Duesenberg chassis was its Lycoming-built, double-overhead-cam, 32-valve, straight-eight engine, producing 265 hp at 4200 rpm. Bore and stroke measured 3.8 inches by 4.8, for a displacement of 420 cubic inches (6.9 liters). A speed of 90 mph could be reached in the middle gear of the three-speed transmission, with a top speed of 116 mph. The chassis came in two wheelbase configurations, 143 and 154 inches. ■ The Model J shown here is an outstanding example of a Murphy town car built on the 154-inch chassis, one of twelve from the Pasadena, California, firm. With 32,000 miles on the odometer, the car is still completely original, right down to the paint, and is believed to be the most pristine example in existence. Its original owner was band leader Paul Whiteman. ■ In 1937, beset by financial problems, Cord sold his empire, effectively killing the Duesenberg. Its demise was not seen by Fred, however, who five years earlier, at the age of 54, never recovered from an accident in one of his own cars. Thus ended the career of one of the greatest names in automotive engineering.

MAYBACH

TYP W6 DSG CABRIOLET

■ The least-known among the great European classics, May-bach—manufactured in Friedrichshafen, Germany—carries a particular aura of exclusivity, a distinction that resulted from the limited numbers produced, the uncompromising devotion to quality that characterized their maker and from the substantial price that typically accompanies low-volume production. ■ In a ranking of exclusivity among prewar German luxury automobiles, one would find Mercedes-Benz next to the top, with Horch a notch below. The unchallenged champion would be Maybach—the automobile for the mature gentleman of means who thought the Mercedes-Benz a bit too flamboyant and the Horch a touch too pedestrian. ■ Another aspect of the Maybach aura stems from the complexity of its engineering—a perfect example of the term "over-engineered." The most vivid illustration of excess could be found in its transmission. After having favored a gearbox with just two forward gears since entering automobile manufacture in 1921, Maybach went overboard with its 1929 model, endowing it with a three-speed unit, which, when augmented with an overdrive that could be activated in any gear—including reverse—allowed six forward choices and two reverse. ■ The system was labelled "Schnell-gang," which translates to "Quick-Shift." The extreme development of this complex device came with the "Doppelschnellgang"

or "Double-Quick-Shift," which, in its ultimate form, offered a choice of eight forward speeds and, theoretically, eight reverse.

■ Perhaps the most epic aspect of the Maybach story stems from its Zeppelin connection. The founder of the Maybach works, Wilhelm Maybach, at first concentrated on the manufacture of engines. This led to a venture with Graf Ferdinand von Zeppelin and his dirigibles, for which Maybach's firm supplied motive power. In 1929, at the height of the Zeppelin era, the globe-encircling airship was propelled by no less than five 550-hp Maybach V-12s. These units inspired the firm's automotive V-12, which, duly mounted in an enormous chassis, received the revered Zeppelin appellation.

■ The Maybach W6 featured on these pages—its Spohn-built body resting on a 144-inch wheelbase—is identical to the mighty Zeppelin in every aspect, except that its hood hides a straight six, a detail that cut the Zeppelin's chassis-only price of $8000 in half. Bore and stroke of the 7.0-liter (427-cubic-inch) unit is 94 mm by 168, with an output of 120 hp at 2200 rpm. ■ The W6 range was offered between 1930 and 1937; some 100 were built, but only three copies of the cabriolet bodystyle featured in the Collection are known to have survived. Two decades of Maybach production, from 1921 to 1941, resulted in approximately 2300 examples—just enough to sustain its exclusivity.

BUGATTI

TYPE 57 AERODYNAMIQUE

■ With an address like "Automobiles E. Bugatti, Molsheim, Bas-Rhin, Alsace," the exotic nature of the product originating from this village in Northern France was established right at the doorstep. Further marvels met the visitor as he proceeded beyond the gates. ■ Not only had Ettore Bugatti built an impressive factory in Alsace-Lorraine, close to the German border, but also vineyards, riding stables and even an inn where customers were accommodated in grand style; through all that surrounded "Le Patron" had to flow "Le Pur Sang"—the pure blood. ■ Born in Milan, Italy, in 1881, Ettore Bugatti was raised by a family of artists— no wonder that the cars he set out to build in 1909 were works of art. The next two decades saw a stream of masterpieces emerge from Molsheim. Foremost among them were such classics as the Type 35, a dominant force on the Grand Prix circuits of the day, and the Type 41—"La Royale"—with its unsurpassed magnificence. ■ By the mid-Thirties, the idyllic tranquility of Molsheim had been exchanged for an atmosphere of confrontation. Nationwide worker unrest had reached the region, and "Le Patron" had fled to Paris in bitter disappointment. The Type 57, which was to embody the best of fast long-distance motoring, had barely been completed. It was up to Ettore's son, Jean, to continue the work. The son proved no less an artist than the father, and, even though some of the

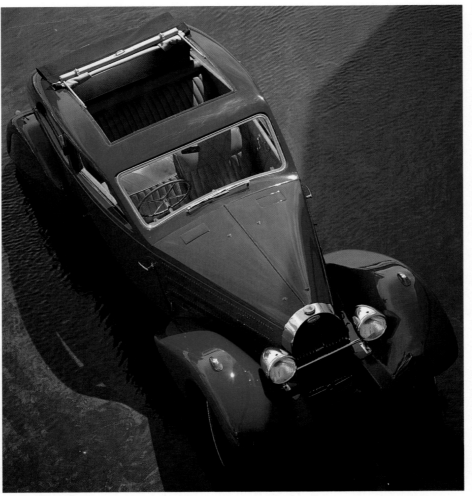

Bugatti's endearing mechanical eccentricity wilted away under Jean's regime, the beauty of his creations have given them a special stature. ■ The Collection's Type 57 represents the more sedate aspects of Jean's production but still illustrates the unique line that flew from his pen. Its two-door, four-seat body was built at Molsheim, as were most of the closed Type 57 bodies. ■ The straight-eight, double overhead-cam engine that powers this Type 57 has a bore and stroke of 72 mm by 100, a displacement of 3.3 liters (200 cubic inches) and an output of 140 hp at 4800 rpm— producing a top speed of around 100 mph. Its 130-inch wheelbase chassis weighs 2100 pounds. ■ In contrast to previous Bugatti practice, the Type 57 had its four-speed, constant-mesh gearbox mounted at the rear of the engine—no longer in unit with the rear axle. Less than 710 were built of the various Type 57 versions, which later included the 57C, 57S and the 57SC. ■ The Type 57 remained in production until 1939, when Jean, swerving to avoid a drunken bicyclist, was killed during the testing of a racer. Later, the factory was taken over by the Germans; the hallowed halls that once housed exotic cars were now subverted to the manufacture of amphibious vehicles and torpedoes. ■ After the war, Ettore attempted to launch the Type 73, but the project died with the death of "Le Patron" in 1947.

CADILLAC

SERIES 90 V-16 TOURING SEDAN

■ The far-reaching effects of the Crash slowly began to ebb by the late Thirties. Yet though the economy was on the upswing and Americans were returning to work, the opulence that had reached its zenith just as the market was reaching its nadir would never be seen again. ■ As the Depression spiraled downward, it took most of the great marques with it: Duesenberg, Cord and Auburn were gone by 1937, as were Marmon and Peerless. And Packard was mortally wounded by the time its production lines were turned over to building PT boat engines. Only Cadillac and Lincoln would survive the war in fighting trim. ■ In February 1933, Cadillac President Lawrence P. Fisher announced that V-16 production would be limited to 400 cars that year, but the bad times called his bluff and only 338 emerged between 1933 and 1937. ■ The original Cadillac V-16 was a jewel-like powerplant befitting "The Standard of the World," but it was also one of the most complex, incorporating some 3300 parts. When Nicholas Dreystadt, formerly Cadillac's general manager of parts and service, took over from Fisher in 1934, he knew the importance of the V-16 to Cadillac's exclusivity—but he also knew the cost of its complexity. ■ One way to simplify it was to take advantage of the manufacturing techniques developed for Cadillac's 1936 V-8 that allowed the crankcase and cylinder block to be cast as a single unit. Another was to eliminate

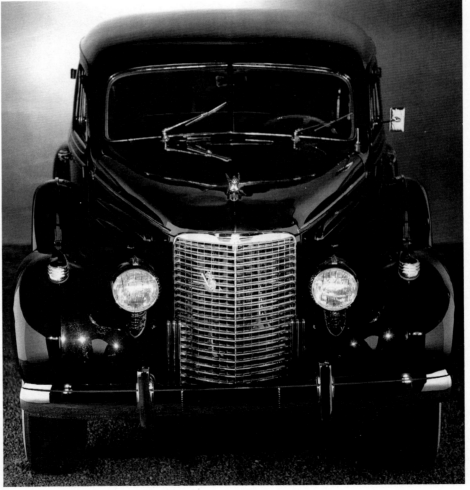

the separate intake manifolds and carburetors by spreading the angle of the cylinder banks from 45 degrees to an unprecedented 135, allowing for a single manifold to be inserted between them while maintaining an angle that would deliver Cadillac's characteristic smoothness. In addition to using fewer parts, the new engine's stroke was reduced to 3.3 inches, while its bore was enlarged to the same distance. The result was a minor decrease in displacement from 452 cubic inches to 431 (7.1 liters) but a weight savings of 250 pounds. Output was largely unchanged, 185 bhp at 3800 rpm. ■ It would not be until 1940 that W.C. Fields would team with Mae West for the film "My Little Chickadee," but the two already had something in common in 1938: an appreciation for the new Cadillac Sixteens that went on sale in October 1937. Miss West made hers a seven-passenger formal sedan, but Fields would buy two: a two-door coupe and the seven-passenger sedan seen here that was later acquired by the Collection. Fields, well-known for his like of liquid refreshment, installed bars in both, with an electric martini mixer in the latter. ■ As with all other Sixteens that year, both cars rode on 141-inch wheelbases. Prices started at $5100 and climbed as high as $7200, small change for a man who so mistrusted banks that he deposited his generous earnings in over 700 accounts around the country.

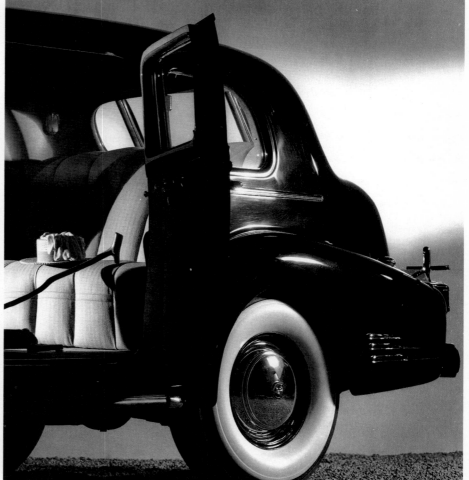

CORD

MODEL 812 PHAETON

On a clear day in the fall of 1940, workers along the road from Tucson to Phoenix suddenly became aware of a plume of dust in the distance. There was nothing unusual about that—the road was just a trail of packed sand in those days—but this time, as the cloud came closer, its vortex approaching at a breakneck speed, the car did not slow down. As the crew scrambled to safety, the yellow monster smashed through the barriers at the work site. Swerving wildly, the car plowed headlong into the ditch the workers had been digging, overturned and crushed its driver. Tom Mix, hero of the silver screen, lay dead at the age of 60.

Today, the monument that marks the spot of Mix's demise also serves as an epitaph of sorts for the car he was driving, a Cord 812, which had met its own demise three years earlier. The seed that grew into the 810 Cord had been sown by Gordon Buehrig in sketches dated November 7, 1933. Here his fertile mind had formulated plans for a futuristic automobile, with a sealed engine compartment flanked by outrigger radiators that snuggled between separate pontoon fenders. The 810 had been conceived as a "baby Duesenberg," but Buehrig's work on the Auburn Boattail Speedster placed the project in limbo. Back on the board, Buehrig refined his sketches into a patent drawing, which was registered on October 2, 1934. The on-again off-

again project received the go-ahead in July of 1935. Its introduction was set for November 2 at the New York Auto Show, which left less than four months to develop a prototype and build 100 examples. Against all odds, the task was accomplished, but—thanks to the cars having been built by hand—the cost grew so high that it spelled the beginning of the end. Mechanically, the 810 Cord was inspired by its front-wheel-drive predecessor, the L-29. This time the engine was a 90-degree V-8, designed for Cord by Lycoming's Forest Baster. Bore and stroke measured 3.5 inches by 3.8, for a displacement of 289 cubic inches (4.7 liters) and an output of 125 hp at 3500 rpm. Its four-speed transmission, featuring electro-vacuum activated gear selection via a lever on the steering column, was located ahead of the engine. The 810's wheelbase was 125 inches, weight 3650 pounds and top speed 90 mph. Available originally in four bodystyles starting at $1995, the 810 was superseded in 1937 by the $2445 812, whose optional supercharger increased output to 170 hp and top speed to 110 mph. The Cord featured in the Collection is the actual car in which Tom Mix met his maker. It was sold wrecked to R. E. Nelson on October 3, 1942 for $100. Restored, it still features Mix's gun holster, as well as his oversized gas pedal, which he unfortunately had a habit of keeping pressed to the floor.

MERCEDES-BENZ

TYP G4 GELANDEWAGEN

■ In the early Thirties, as the Third Reich was cranking up its war machinery, a number of German concerns saw an increasing share of their capacity devoted to military production. The most prestigious of the automakers, Daimler-Benz, was no exception. ■ In 1934, the company unveiled a remarkable six-wheeler designated G4. The "G" stood for "gelände," German for cross-country. The vehicle was intended for command use, but experience in the field revealed that its excessive weight—well over 8000 pounds—made its fitness for this type of work questionable—despite the added traction of its four rugged rear wheels. Instead, the G4's primary role became that of a parade vehicle for party dignitaries. ■ Regardless of its utilization, the G4 represented automotive engineering at its best. It was built in the mold of the contemporary Grosser Mercedes, but used the 5.0-liter (305-cubic-inch) engine from the 500K, later updated to the 540K's 5.4-liter (330-cubic-inch) motor. In the latter configuration, the overhead-valve, straight-eight produced 115 hp at 2000 rpm. ■ Because of the G4's original mandate as an off-road vehicle, it did not share the 500/540K's on-demand supercharger. Coupled to a suitably geared four-speed transmission—equipped with two reverse ratios—the engine generated a top speed of 50 mph. Up front the 160-inch-wheelbase chassis displayed standard Mercedes fare,

while in the rear, rigid axles replaced swing axles. ■ If the engineers went all out, so did the coachbuilders. Seating was for seven; two up front, two on folding chairs in the middle, and three on a rear bench. Sumptuous leather covered all surfaces. Leather was also used in the trunk, where the occupants could stow their belongings in fitted luggage. ■ A total of 57 units were built between 1934 and 1939. One of the last G4s was presented to Generalissimo Franco and still remains with the Spanish state. Only three additional examples are known to have survived. ■ The G4 acquired by the Collection was delivered to the German Army High Command on September 6, 1938, as duly noted on a factory document. A curious addendum suggests that the vehicle might have been diverted to the personal use of Mussolini; it seems the G4 was transported to Genoa on August 27, 1939, for further shipment to Tripoli, Libya—then under Italian occupation. ■ The tracks made by the G4 as it found its way to Los Angeles after the war have long since been obliterated. For many years it belonged to Pacific Auto Rental, a company supplying vehicles to the movie industry. In this capacity, it played many a starring role, including an appearance in the television series "Hogan's Heroes." ■ It was subsequently restored to its original splendor by the craftsmen of the Collection's own restoration shop.

■ THE GARGANTUAN G4 WAS OFTEN UNDONE BY ITS OWN WEIGHT

ALFA ROMEO

TIPO 6C 2500S BERLINETTA

■ When a car that represents the pinnacle of both a manufacturer and a coachbuilder also plays a role in world events, it assures for itself an important place in automotive history. The Collection's Alfa Romeo is such a car. ■ Società Anonima Lombarda Fabbrica Automobili—Alfa for short—was formed in Milan in 1910. An improved version of the firm's first car entered the 1911 Targa Florio, establishing Alfa's racing credentials right from the start. ■ After World War I, Nicola Romeo's investment in the firm added his name to the badge and initiated a steady flow of fabulous machines. The Vittorio Jano-designed 6C 1500 and its successors confirmed the greatness of the marque, compiling countless racing victories. ■ Concurrent with its sports cars, Alfa Romeo also built Grand Prix racers. The P2 captured the 1925 World Championship for Manufacturers, adding a laurel wreath to the Alfa badge. The subsequent P3 won every Grand Prix of the 1932 season—one of the most impressive feats in racing history. In the late Thirties came the culmination of the road Alfas, the fabulous 8C 2900—the fastest production car of its day. Also emerging at this high point was the 6C 2500. ■ The "two-five's" exquisite powerplant was a straight six, sporting double overhead cams and hemispherical combustion chambers. Bore and stroke were 72 mm by 100, displacement 2.5 liters (150 cubic inches) and output 95 hp at 4600 rpm, for a top speed of 100 mph. Suspension was independent all around, brakes were four-wheel drums and transmission four-speed non-synchromesh. The advanced chassis, with its 118-inch wheelbase, formed a worthy foundation for a dramatic body created by Carrozzeria Touring. ■ Beginning in 1926, Felice Bianchi Anderloni and his Touring firm made their mark with its classic clothing for sports cars in general, Alfas in particular. Starting in 1937, the firm augmented coachbuilding technology with its patented "Superleggera" or "superlight" system that replaced traditional wood body framing with a light tubular steel skeleton covered by a thin aluminum skin. ■ The collection's Alfa—one of 66 S-versions built, of which half were fitted with the Touring body—was a gift from Mussolini to his mistress Clara Petacci. As the Allied forces in Italy tied an ever-tightening knot around the dictator, he and his mistress decided to make a dash for the Swiss border, using the Alfa for the escape. Not far from their destination, however, they were apprehended and executed. ■ The Alfa spent some time impounded by the local police before an American soldier brought it to the U.S. Today, its history verified by Petacci's wartime bodyguard, this survivor stands resurrected by the Collection's own restoration shop—a symbol of automotive design at its best and a memento of a tragic chapter in history.

PACKARD

MODEL 1605 SUPER EIGHT

■ Packard, unlike so many of its colleagues, managed to weather the Depression—but not without a tarnished image. Financial survival had meant giving up some of the exclusivity that had built its enviable image. ■ In 1932, alarmed by dwindling sales, Packard introduced the Light-Eight, an "economy car." It failed to attract the desired customers, however, and was discontinued the same year. The 120, announced in 1935, was another attempt at a lower-priced model, and this time the approach succeeded. By 1937, when the 120 reached the market in full force, annual production soared to a record level of nearly 50,000 units. ■ For 1938, the Packard line consisted of the Six, the Eight, the Super Eight and, at the top of the ladder, the Twelve. It was an orderly hierarchy that spanned the spectrum from relative economy, with prices beginning at $975 for a Six Business Coupe, to definitive extravagance, with $8510 for a V-12 Touring Cabriolet by Brunn. ■ Regardless of its flirtation with the masses, Packard remained a favorite with the upper crust—a fact underscored by the many rich and famous who chose Packards for their transportation. Not only was the leader of the free world, Franklin Delano Roosevelt, partial to America's premier luxury car, but dictators in particular seemed to have a propensity for Packards, as illustrated by Stalin's Super Eight Convertible Sedan, and by the Collection's Super Eight—a

dual-cowl Phaeton bodied by the Rosemont, Pennsylvania firm of Derham—was previously owned by Argentine strongman Juan Perón. ■ Compared to the angular styling of the early Thirties, the look of the late Thirties was characterized by smoothly streamlined fenders and all-enveloping bodies. Packard followed the trend, but slowly. Its headlights, for instance, were still mounted on the exterior, in the classic mode—although they had now taken on the fashionable teardrop shape. A further concession to the aerodynamic vogue was the introduction of a vee-shaped windshield. ■ The Super Eight received its power from Packard's familiar straight-eight, now with a bore and stroke of 3.2 inches by 5.0, a displacement of 320 cubic inches (5.2 liters) and an output of 130 hp at 3200 rpm—a powerplant giving smooth and effortless propulsion at any speed. Its refinement was further enhanced by a selective-synchromesh three-speed transmission. The Super Eight's ride was already smooth, but improved further with a semi-floating rear axle. The weight of the Derham Phaeton—resting on a 151-inch wheelbase—was around 5000 pounds and the price in the $10,000 range. ■ The next two decades saw Packard decline steadily towards its regrettable extinction. During the late Thirties—in the last throes of the classic era—however, the top-of-the-line Packards revealed few signs of fading glory.

GRAHAM

MODEL 97 FOUR-DOOR SEDAN

■ After a spectacular rise to prominence in the late Twenties, when annual production hit a high of 73,000 units, the post-Crash Thirties found Graham in need of a shot in the arm. Styling and supercharging were the potions expected to do the trick. While, in the end, neither had the desired effect, the effort produced a memorable product. ■ The Graham had its roots in a company called Paige-Detroit, founded in 1909. By the outbreak of World War I, "Detroit" had been dropped, and the Paige name alone adorned a range of new designs. ■ In 1927, the company was taken over by the Graham brothers, who had made their mark and their money in a joint venture with another brother team, the Dodges. The Paige badge now received the addition of the Graham name, becoming the Graham-Paige. By 1930 the Paige portion was dropped. ■ Graham's supercharger was introduced in 1934—a first for a moderately-priced car—and made the straight-eight Blue Streak worthy of its name; top speed was in the 95 mph range. As with the Duesenberg supercharger, the Graham version was of the centrifugal type and improved mid-range performance. ■ Although production had risen from a low of 11,000 in 1933 to 21,000 in 1937, the Graham brothers were not satisfied. They returned to Amos Northup, who had been responsible for the styling of the Blue Streak. Northup came through with an extraordinary effort, christened the "Sharknose." While Gordon Buehrig's ground-breaking design for the 810 Cord—which itself was nicknamed the "Coffin Nose"—adhered to the principle of "form follows function," Northup's design drew its inspiration from trends in the decorative arts. ■ Introduced in 1938, the Sharknose was available only as a four-door sedan; Model 96 was unsupercharged, Model 97 supercharged, the latter priced from $1198. Under the skin, the frame was redesigned to allow a lower profile, although the engine was essentially unchanged: an L-head six with a bore and stroke of 3.3 inches by 4.4, and a displacement of 218 cubic inches (3.6 liters). Output for the supercharged version was 120 hp, which propelled the 3300-pound car to 60 mph in 16 seconds. Its four-speed transmission incorporated a fuel-saving overdrive. ■ Although an aesthetic triumph, the Sharknose did not go over well with the public; the Graham organization dipped into the red. While further desperate efforts at recovery were made, the last automotive breath had been drawn by 1940. With the war, the factory turned to military production. ■ Today, the Sharknose cuts a startling figure on the Collection floor, where its radical front end—perhaps the most extreme of the Art Deco era—has earned it the same prominent place it holds in the annals of automotive design.

PACKARD

MODEL 1708 TOURING CABRIOLET

■ Nineteen thirty-nine was a watershed year for Packard. Not only did the company celebrate its fortieth anniversary—although with scarcely a mention, except by the press—but the year also marked the end of the magnificent Twelve, the last of the Senior Packards. Also that year, the company began producing its twelve-cylinder PT boat engine for the Navy—an ominous sign of the dark period to come. ■ The most outstanding of the classic Packards—the V-12-powered Ninth to Seventeenth Series—had been introduced in 1932 as the Packard Twin Six, although its designation was changed to Packard Twelve the following year. ■ Work on the V-12 powerplant had commenced in 1930, when Cornelius Van Ranst, a brilliant engineer of Cord L-29 fame, was hired by Packard on a contract basis. Van Ranst's brief had actually called for him to develop a front-wheel-drive V-12 chassis, but by the time a prototype—which eventually ran at speeds of 110 mph on the Packard proving grounds—had been completed, management had opted for a conventional layout. ■ In its original configuration, the Van Ranst V-12, a 67-degree, modified-L-head design, featured a bore and stroke of 3.4 inches by 3.5, a displacement of 375 cubic inches (6.1 liters) and an output of 150 hp at 3500 rpm. For a multi-cylinder engine, it was a small package, originally intended to power a new mid-size line of Packards. Instead, this marvel of smoothness, duly increased in displacement, was mated to one of the most sophisticated Packards ever built. ■ By the time it reached production as the 1932 Twin Six, the Packard V-12 had had its bore and stroke increased to 3.4 inches by 4.0, which resulted in a displacement of 446 cubic inches (7.3 liters) and an output of 160 hp at 3200 rpm. The specifications were changed again in 1935 with the introduction of the Twelfth Series to 3.4 inches by 4.3, 473 cubic inches (7.8 liters) and 175 hp at 3200 rpm. ■ For 1939, the year of the Collection's choice—a Brunn-built, 139-inch wheelbase Touring Cabriolet weighing some 5845 pounds and priced at $8355—the Twelve's basic specifications remained unchanged: three-speed transmission with vacuum-controlled free-wheeling; vacuum-boosted, twin-shoe Bendix brakes; pressed-steel frame with X-shaped center brace channels; and independent front suspension. ■ During the last year of production, just 280 V-12s were built, of which less than a dozen were bodied by Brunn. These top-of-the-line Packards were favorites of numerous world leaders; the Collection's example, armor-plated to resist 50-caliber machine gun bullets, was used by a succession of Mexican Presidents. Still wearing appropriate seals and flags, this impressive survivor remains unrestored, a magnificent reminder of the last great Packard.

DELAHAYE

TYPE 175S AERODYNAMIQUE

■ Spanning half a tumultuous century, the Delahaye story represents legend-building on a grand scale. At the introduction of the epic appears Emile Delahaye, an engineer from Tours, France, whose place among the pioneers was secured by virtue of the automobile he built in 1895. ■ Despite his pioneering role, Delahaye, who died in 1905, never became the grand master of his own marque. That title belongs to Charles Weiffenbach, known among his peers as Monsieur Charles. Joining the firm at the turn of the century, he remained at the helm until Delahaye closed its doors in 1954. ■ Over the years, Monsieur Charles expanded the Delahaye name to represent not only an armada of passenger cars, but also trucks and fire engines. In the early Thirties, however, the creative spirit seemed to have left him; Delahayes lost their distinctive edge, sending the fortunes of the marque into a tailspin.

■ Then, in 1933, inspired it is said by Ettore Bugatti, Weiffenbach launched a breathtaking crop of high-performance machines. The following year, a Delahaye broke seven world records at Montlhéry. Further victories secured soaring sales and renewed prosperity. Adding to the Delahaye grandeur during this period were the fabulous bodies bestowed on them by France's most famous coachbuilders, Figoni et Falaschi foremost among them.

■ Giuseppe Figoni, an Italian, had arrived in Paris with his parents

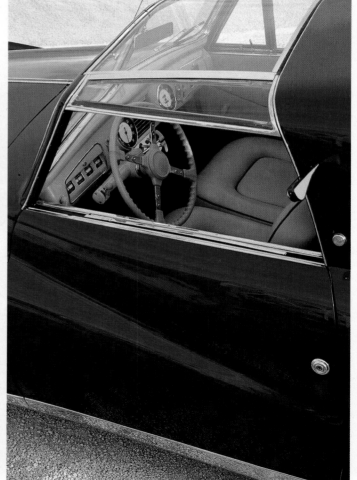

at the turn of the century. After serving his apprenticeship in a wagon builder's shop, the young man soon set up his own coachbuilding works in the fashionable suburb of Boulogne-Sur-Seine. By 1935, Figoni—the artist—had acquired a style that set automobile enthusiasts on fire. He had also acquired a partner, fellow Italian Ovidio Falaschi—the businessman. ■ The five-seat Delahaye seen on these pages is the prototype of Monseiur Charles' first postwar model and an outstanding example of Figoni at his best. In addition to its flowing lines—the aerodynamic appearance based more on artistic interpretation than empirical research—the design features a remarkably futuristic removable glass roof. ■ Below the seductive skin hides a 4.5-liter (275-cubic-inch), 140-hp straight-six with a bore and stroke of 94 mm by 107. The 132-inch wheelbase chassis rests on Dubonnet independent suspension up front and a de Dion axle at the rear. The four-speed transmission features the Cotal semi-automatic preselector system. ■ Restored to perfection, this one-off Delahaye represents the zenith of the coachbuilder's craft—and the end of an era. The cost of handcraftsmanship had climbed too high in an age of mass production. By 1951, the Type 175 had been replaced by the Type 235, a model that lacked the excitement of the past and failed to stem the company's slide towards its 1954 extinction.

TUCKER

MODEL 48 FOUR-DOOR SEDAN

■ More than any other automobile, the Tucker represents the entrepreneurial free-for-all of early postwar America. Even before Preston Tucker and his car became heroes of the big screen, there were many whose emotions stirred at the recollection of the super-promoter introducing "The First New Car in Fifty Years." ■ Perhaps, if being a bully has something to do with bullishness, Tucker's background as both a car salesman and a policeman might explain the aggressiveness with which he pursued his goals. ■ Tucker's first automotive effort involved Harry Miller, with whom he developed plans for a rear-engined sports car called the Torpedo. Although the project was abandoned, out of it grew greater ambitions. Tucker now wanted to build a car for the masses, an automobile so advanced it would knock the breath out of both the public and the established manufacturers. ■ Tucker turned to stylist Alex Tremulis, who, expanding on the Torpedo, created a new design in one week. Sketches in hand, Tucker proceeded to raise capital through a stock issue that attracted 44,000 shareholders. He also signed up dealers, leased production facilities and even went as far as selling accessory kits—for cars that didn't yet exist. ■ The fact that nothing more than a prototype had been built soon became a source of dubious speculation; a 100-day crash program produced fifty examples. Displayed around the

country, these pilots provided tangible proof that the Tucker was indeed the most advanced car of its time. ■ The streamlined body featured three headlights, the center "Cyclops" lamp turning with the wheels for safer operation at night. A host of other safety features included a windshield that popped out on impact. Below the space-age surface, the 4235-pound car sported all-independent suspension on a 128-inch wheelbase. The transmission was a vacuum-operated, four-speed manual unit, but production cars were to receive an automatic version. ■ The rear-mounted engine was a flat, opposed six, developed for helicopter use by Air-Cooled Motors. The overhead-valve, oversquare unit—converted to water cooling—had a bore and stroke of 4.5 inches by 3.5, a displacement of 334 cubic inches (5.5 liters) and an output of 166 hp at 3200 rpm. Top speed was 110 mph. And it could be yours for $2450. ■ But then the Federal watchdogs entered the act. Charged with securities violations, Tucker was indicted for fraud. His trial ended in acquittal, but by then the momentum was lost. Tucker sought vindication in his book "My Car Was Too Good." Perhaps, with time, it could have been good. Burdened by a 58 percent rear bias, however, it is doubtful that the handling could ever have become acceptable. ■ As a collector car the Tucker has shown remarkable longevity; of the 51 built, 49 remain.

MERCEDES-BENZ

TYP 770K OFFENER TOURENWAGEN

■ As the Third Reich and its megalomaniacal leadership marched inexorably towards its apocalyptic climax, the might of its muscle—as far as automotive preference was concerned—was manifested by the Grosser Mercedes, produced in two generations from 1930 to 1943. ■ The unforgettable images of imperious party dignitaries plying the oceans of mass hysteria in their conveyances of steel and rubber made the Grosser Mercedes an inseparable part of the lore of the Third Reich. Yet the deplorable elements of this dark era were certainly not the inanimate objects, but rather their diabolical occupants. ■ First shown at the 1938 Berlin auto show, the second-generation Grosser Mercedes—by then reserved for party dignitaries—was quite different from its 1930-38 predecessor of the same name. Referred to by Daimler-Benz as the W 150, the 770K sported a completely new chassis with independent suspension both front and rear. ■ Power still came from the 7.7 liter straight eight—its black-lacquer exterior subtly complemented by chrome accessories and engine-turned alloy surfaces—with its bore and stroke of 95 mm by 135. Thanks to increased compression, however, the output now reached a supercharged maximum of 230 hp at 3200 rpm. The transmission remained unchanged except for the addition of a fifth gear. ■ The Grosser Mercedes—"gross" meaning big in German—would reach its peak with the W 150. Its wheelbase had grown by 5 inches to 155 inches, the overall length by 16 inches to 240 inches. A handful of vehicles received armor plating, which increased weight by some 2000 pounds. Also part of this package was bullet-proof window glass, as well as special tires whose two dozen separate chambers limited damage when punctured.

■ Some automotive historians suggest that a very few of these armor-plated giants received special treatment under the hood. The added weight certainly called for added power, and more efficient breathing would have been the answer. This was accomplished with four valves per cylinder, two twin-throat carburetors and double superchargers, features that would have upped output to a stunning 400 hp at 3600 rpm—enough to propel the mastodon to speeds in excess of 110 mph. ■ Altogether, 88 units were built —the special vehicles included. The example featured here—a single-supercharger, non-bulletproofed version—was delivered in 1943 to the Führer's personal retreat in Berchtesgaden. The Collection also has on display the only automobile that specifically mentions the Führer's name on its registration documents. ■ Regardless of their sinister application, these automobiles, with their brilliant engineering, compelling proportions and magnificent craftsmanship, represent one of the high points in automotive history.

MUNTZ

JET CONVERTIBLE COUPE

■ Nothing stirs the appetite quite as much as having to do without. The Thirties and Forties robbed a generation of its right to pursuit of prosperity; the Depression, leaving lurid snapshots of misery, was followed by the attack on Pearl Harbor, forcing the nation into yet another period of denial. By 1945, Americans were desperate for the trappings of affluence. ■ Nothing embodies the good life quite as much as the automobile, and soon makers were scrambling to meet the pent-up demand. In this climate, two talented men—an engineer and a salesman—both operating out of Glendale, California, would make names for themselves. ■ Frank Kurtis, the engineer, was already a successful manufacturer of midget racers. In 1948, he turned to another project, a sporty two-seater. Built from off-the-shelf components, the Kurtis was nothing more than an assembled car—and an expensive one at that. Only some thirty-six were built during 1948 and 1949. ■ Earl Muntz, the salesman, was a prodigy. At the age of eight, he assembled and sold radios. At twenty, he owned a used-car lot in Elgin, Illinois. Soon, booming Southern California beckoned. There, back in the used-car business, "Madman Muntz"—aided by outrageous radio commercials—earned both a fortune and a nickname. In 1947, entering the big league, he launched his own brand of black-and-white TVs. ■ Flush with capital, Muntz bought the Kurtis opera-

tion for $200,000. Retaining the basic shape of the car, he made room for a rear seat by stretching the wheelbase to 113 inches. Cadillac's 331-cubic-inch (5.4-liter) overhead-valve V-8, with a bore and stroke of 3.8 inches by 3.6 and an output of 160 hp, became standard power, producing a top speed of 110 mph and a 0-to-60 mph time of 8 seconds flat. Renamed the Muntz Jet and sporting the "Madman" symbol on the horn button, the revamped car stood ready for sale in 1950. ■ After building twenty-eight Jets in his Glendale plant, Muntz moved the operation to Evanston, Illinois, where he cut costs through improved production methods. The wheelbase was stretched again, to 116 inches, the aluminum body changed to steel, a choice of Lincoln power added, and the original Hydra-matic augmented by a three-speed manual with Borg-Warner overdrive. ■ Muntz's clever advertising brought customers, but in spite of the $5200 price he lost $1000 per car and abandoned the project in 1954. Production estimates vary between 200 and 400. Later, with the arrival of color TV, the Muntz empire suffered another setback. Frank Kurtis, on the other hand, became the Fifties' most successful builder of Indianapolis racers. ■ Today, the Collection's Glendale-built Muntz stands as a rare reminder of an effort that, in spite of its maverick spirit, paved the way for the American sports car.

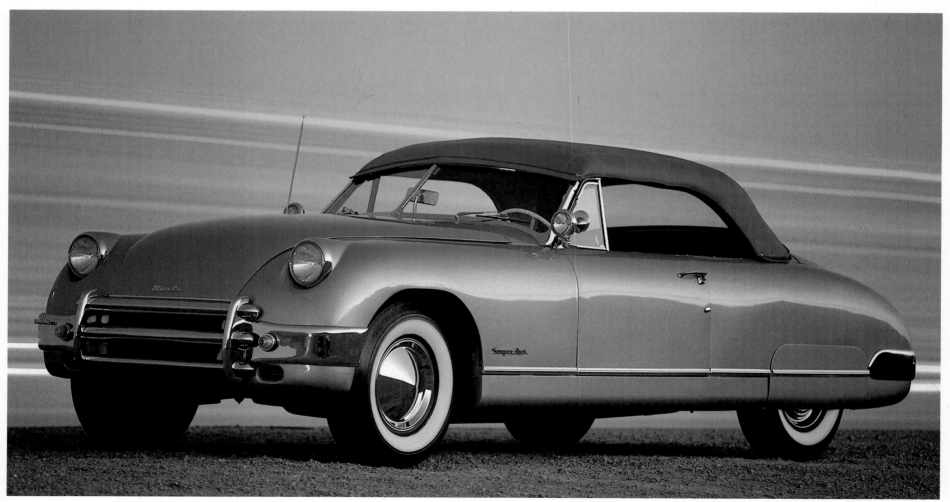

NASH

AMBASSADOR CUSTOM

■ The fortunes of Nash were shaped by three men, all masters in the game of survival. Abandoned by his parents at the age of six, Charles Nash learned to fend for himself the hard way. By the time he was thirty-one, he had risen to the vice-presidency of Durant-Dort; at forty-eight, he was president of General Motors. ■ A falling out with Billy Durant led to Nash's buying the Jeffrey Company in 1916. The following year saw the Nash badge for the first time, affixed to virtually unchanged Jeffreys. ■ Nash introduced his first eight-cylinder car in 1929, managing a $7.6 million profit in a Depression-ravaged 1930. By 1933 the bad times had caught up, however, and only 15,000 were sold, causing a loss of $1.2 million. By the mid-Thirties, Nash had regained its momentum—in 1936, sales zoomed to 53,000 and kept soaring. ■ With all indicators on the rise, Nash began searching for a successor. His choice fell on George Mason, president of Kelvinator. Mason was interested—but only if he could take the refrigerator manufacturer with him. Nash assented, and in 1937, Nash and Kelvinator became a strange but viable alliance, and Nash retired to his Beverly Hills mansion. ■ As a boy, George Mason picked mustard for fifty cents a week. As a young man, he sold cars for fifty dollars a month. An engineering degree landed him jobs with Studebaker and Dodge. After a stint in banking, he returned to cars, now with

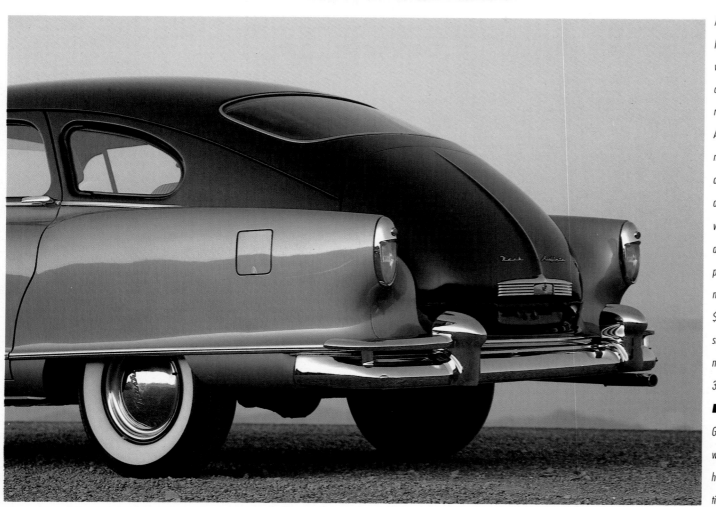

Maxwell and Chrysler, before taking over at Kelvinator. ■ As the head of the independent Nash, Mason knew he needed products with a distinctive look. The answer, the Airflyte series, was introduced in 1948, the year Charlie Nash died. Inspired by a wartime model sculpted by Ted Pietsch and Holden Koto, some thought the Airflyte resembled a spaceship, others a bath tub. Among their innovations was a body featuring advanced unit construction as well as reclining front seats. Nash said the seats were for sleeping, but an awakening teenage population soon saw other possibilities. For whatever reason, the two cars that made up the series—the 600 and the Ambassador—sold like hotcakes. Nash production peaked at 190,000 units in 1949, generating a tidy profit of $26 million. ■ In 1951, the Ambassador Custom Sedan, priced at $2501, received a new grille. Power came from an overhead-valve six, with a bore and stroke of 3.4 inches by 4.4 inches, a displacement of 235 cubic inches (3.8 liters) and an output of 112 hp at 3400 rpm. Weight was 3445 pounds, wheelbase 121 inches. ■ In 1954, it was Mason's turn to bite the final bullet, and George Romney, his handpicked successor, took over. Romney, who had learned the business by putting on overalls and getting his hands dirty, led Nash into the merger with Hudson, which would ultimately create the foundation of American Motors.

CHRYSLER

IMPERIAL PARADE PHAETON

■ Few occasions lend so much prestige to a vehicle as its majestic descent amid lines of cheering crowds. We think of the flickering images of ticker-tape parades honoring returning heros, the classic hoods and fenders of Marmons and Cadillacs littered with the barometer of Wall Street gone wild. ■ In the early Fifties all this weighed heavily on the shoulders of the men whose responsibility it was to keep Chrysler before the eyes of the people. From General Manager K. T. Keller down the line to the public relations office, it was agreed that putting Chryslers on parade was good publicity. ■ In 1951, Chrysler began building three vehicles for precisely that purpose. These would be headquartered strategically around the country—in New York, Detroit and Los Angeles—and be made available to dignitaries on a request basis. ■ The project was assigned to Chrysler stylist Virgil Exner and his staff—mostly his staff, because Exner was in the midst of a major revamp of the Chrysler lines. Inspiration was taken from the 1941 Newport show cars and their dual-cowl configuration. The chassis were Crown Imperial limousine units, with wheelbases stretched to 147.5 inches, creating an overall length of 241 inches. Stock 1951 Imperial grilles and front and rear bumpers were used to assure identity with the showroom line, but everything in between was all-new.

■ The West Coast car made its debut at the 1953 Tournament of

Roses parade in Pasadena, carrying Grand Marshal and Vice President-elect Richard Nixon. Other dignitaries who revealed themselves to the masses from the seats of the Chrysler ranged from Churchill to Khrushchev. ■ In 1955, the cars were returned to Chrysler for updating. This time, 1956 Crown Imperial front-end sheet metal, including grilles, bumpers, hoods and fenders were mated to the appropriate parts from the rear, including Imperial fenders complete with gun sight tail lights. ■ Power for the 5814-pound behemoths came from Chrysler's overhead-valve V-8 hemi, with a bore and stroke of 3.8 inches by 3.6, a displacement of 331 cubic inches (5.4 liters) and an output of 250 hp at 4600 rpm. Each car used a two-speed Powerflite automatic transmission.

■ Duly revitalized, the cars returned to their respective locations. After years of service, the Los Angeles car was sold to the City of Los Angeles, in whose hands it still remains. The Detroit car was vandalized and had to be scrapped. The New York car saw extensive use in State Department and White House service, on numerous occasions carrying President Eisenhower. In 1964, it was returned to Chrysler and was subsequently acquired by the Collection. Still in its original condition, the magnificent Eisenhower car recalls a time when both automobiles and ceremonial pomp were celebrated on a grand scale.

MERCEDES-BENZ

300SL COUPE

■ In the early Fifties, after the paralysis of the war years, Mercedes-Benz began to yearn for the glory of the past, an era when the supercharged roar of its racing giants sent shock waves of awe across Europe's Grand Prix circuits. The decision to return to racing was more than sentimental, it was logical. What better way to generate interest in a new line of production cars? ■ It fell to veteran engineer Rudolph Uhlenhaut to prepare a car for the great return—no simple task, as he was forced to work with an existing engine, a tall, single-overhead-cam straight-six, designed for the firm's luxury line. Bore and stroke were nearly square, 85 mm by 88, creating a displacement of 3.0 liters (183 cubic inches). Ready to race, it generated 175 hp at 5200 rpm. ■ Uhlenhaut solved the need for a low hood profile by placing the engine at a 45-degree angle. But not only was the engine tall, it was also heavy, requiring Uhlenhaut to come up with an ultralight skeleton. Again, he drew on his talent for the unorthodox, creating a space frame built from a network of small-diameter steel tubes. In order to preserve structural strength, however, the design could not accommodate conventional doors. The solution? Roof-hinged "gullwing" doors. ■ The 300SL—the S standing for Sport, the L for Leicht, meaning light—was first put to the test in the 1952 Mille Miglia, where it lost to a Ferrari. But from then on, the 300SL

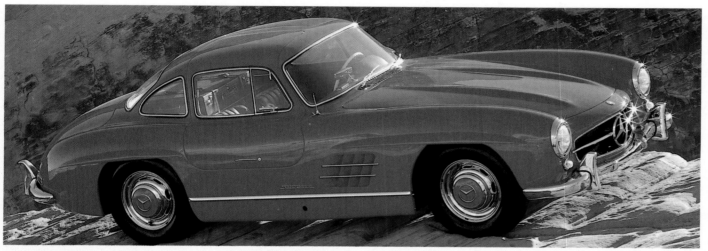

produced a straight flush, winning the Swiss Grand Prix, Le Mans, the German Grand Prix, and finally, the most grueling of them all, La Carrera Panamericana. ■ The story might have ended there, had it not been for the vision of Max Hoffman, New York's super-purveyor of sports cars. He convinced Mercedes to build a road version of the 300SL, backing his enthusiasm with an order for 1000 examples. ■ Uhlenhaut—complemented by Walter Häcker on the styling side—went back to the drawing board. The basics of the racer were kept intact, including its tubular frame and upward-opening doors. The engine also remained, but was fitted with fuel-injection—a first for a gasoline-fueled production engine. This, along with a new cylinder head, upped performance to 240 hp at 4800 rpm. Although civilization increased the 300SL's weight from 1918 pounds to 2700, its top speed was an impressive 140 mph plus—enough to make the 300SL the fastest car of its day. ■ Despite a price that soared to nearly $10,000, Mercedes lost money on the project. After building 146 cars in 1954, 867 in 1955, 311 in 1956, and 76 in 1957, for a total of 1400, the Gullwing—as it was unofficially called—was replaced by a less exciting roadster. ■ Just one step from the race track, the 300SL—a blend of the primitive and the refined—is one of the most striking interpretations of the sports car ideal.

CADILLAC

SERIES 62 CONVERTIBLE

■ After the drudgery of war, the arrival of peace sent Americans on a binge of self-indulgence. With money to spend and a continent to discover, the automobile emerged as the national symbol of freedom and prosperity. ■ Prodded by an appetite that bordered on the insatiable, the limits of taste were continuously tested; the consumer turned from pupil to tutor, and the Fifties became automotive styling's era of excess. ■ The man uniquely equipped to define and exploit these urges was Harley Earl. It seems no coincidence that he was born in Hollywood, the capital of dream imagery. After appropriate schooling, Earl took charge of his father's custom shop, where he built cars for the stars. The mechanisms that would bring on the birth of the Dream Machine were in place. ■ Earl came to Detroit at the urging of Cadillac chief Larry Fisher, whose 1927 LaSalle became Earl's first showcase as well as a harbinger of the type of automobile that established its status primarily on visual appeal. ■ By the end of the war, most luxury automobiles had succumbed to the Crash and its legacy of despair. True, Packard had survived, but its decline had started before the war and could not be stopped. This left Cadillac to emerge as the reigning heir to the luxury car throne. ■ Three decades after Earl arrived at Cadillac, he continued to consolidate its position as a style leader. His 1949 Le Sabre showcar introduced an array of air-

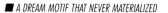

craft-inspired elements, and soon all cars sported bomb sights, bullets and sweep spears. ■ In 1949, Cadillac became the first mass-produced car to incorporate tail fins. The following year, Earl's creed of Lower and Longer brought even greater excitement to the Cadillac line. By 1953, the Eldorado defined a new direction, incorporating a wraparound windshield for the first time on a production car. In 1957, the Eldorado Brougham introduced quad headlights—another first. ■ The standard Cadillac line for 1957 was stylish enough, as illustrated by the Collection's Series 62 Convertible, delectably finished in metallic pink. Exactly 9000 were built, each carrying a sticker price of $5225. Power came from Cadillac's potent 365-cubic-inch (6.0-liter), overhead-valve V-8, with a bore and stroke of 4.0 inches by 3.6 and an output of 300 hp at 4800 rpm. The body, 216 inches long, languished atop a 130-inch wheelbase. Hydra-Matic drive, power steering and power brakes were standard on all Cadillacs. ■ In 1959, General Motors announced Harley Earl's retirement. As he prepared to leave, the 1959 Eldorado Biarritz Convertible—the epitome of Cadillac Fifties styling—arrived on the scene. Featuring Detroit's most outrageous fins ever, conspicuously accented by dual bullet-shaped taillights, the Eldorado was a fitting monument to a man who would be remembered as Detroit's dream maker.